GOING WILD

IN WASHINGTON AND OREGON

SUSAN EWING

Happy Trails!

Susan

Alaska Northwest Books™

Anchorage ◆ Seattle ◆ Portland

To Jessica Maxwell,
wild soul sister and mother of ideas

Library of Congress Cataloging-in-Publication Data
Ewing, Susan, 1954–
    Going wild in Washington and Oregon : seasonal excursions to wildlife
and habitats / by Susan Ewing.
         p.   cm.
    Includes biographical references (p. 220) and index.
    ISBN 0-88240-426-1
    1. Wildlife viewing sites—Washington (State)—Guidebooks.   2. Wildlife viewing
sites—Oregon—Guidebooks.   3. Wildlife watching—Washington (State)—
Guidebooks.   4. Wildlife watching—Oregon (State)—Guidebooks.   5. Natural
history—Washington (State)—Guidebooks.   6. Natural history—Oregon—
Guidebooks.   I. Title.
QL212.E95   1993
599'.09795—dc20   92-45812
                                                   CIP

Managing editor: Ellen Harkins Wheat
Editor: Linda Gunnarson
Book designer: Alice C. Merrill
Cartographer: Vikki Leib

Illustrations by Gretchen Daiber

Cover photo: Roosevelt elk on the Olympic Peninsula, Washington. Photograph by
Art Wolfe/Allstock, Inc.

Credit for sources: The following works are reprinted in this book with permission from
their publishers: The epigraph on p. 5 is from Wendell Berry, *Collected Poems 1957–1982,*
Berkeley, Calif., North Point Press, 1985. The epigraph at the opening of Chapter 8 is
adapted from Richard Erdoes and Alfonso Ortiz, editors, *American Myths and Legends,*
New York, Random House, 1984. The poem partially quoted at the end of Chapter 9 is
from Edward Lear, *The Pelican Chorus,* New York, Parents' Magazine Press, 1967. The
Samish legend quoted in Chapter 10 is adapted from Ella E. Clark, *Indian Legends of the
Pacific Northwest,* Berkeley, University of California Press, 1953.

Alaska Northwest Books™
An imprint of Graphic Arts Center Publishing Company
Editorial office: 2208 NW Market Street, #300, Seattle, WA 98107
Catalog and order dept.: P.O. Box 10306, Portland, OR 97201
   800-452-3032

Printed in the United States of America

CONTENTS

The Peace of Wild Things

When despair for the world grows in me
and I wake in the night at the least sound
in fear of what my life and my children's lives may be,
I go and lie down where the wood drake
rests in his beauty on the water, and the great heron
feeds. I come into the peace of wild things
who do not tax their lives with forethought
of grief. I come into the presence of still water.
And I feel above me the day-blind stars
waiting with their light. For a time
I rest in the grace of the world, and am free.

—Wendell Berry

WILDLIFE TRIPS IN WASHINGTON AND OREGON

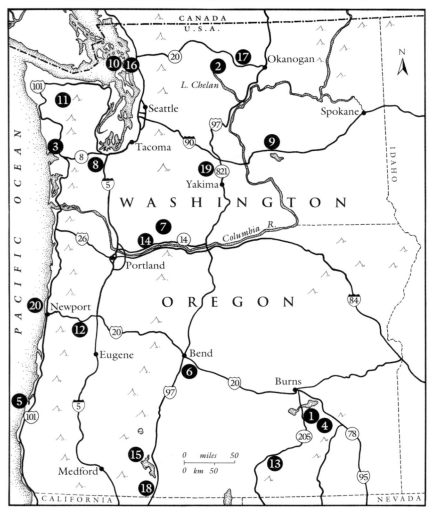

1. Sandhill Cranes
2. Wildlife Sampler
3. Shorebirds
4. Mustangs
5. Seals/Sea Lions
6. Bats
7. Frogs/Salamanders
8. Butterflies
9. White Pelicans
10. Tidepools
11. Roosevelt Elk
12. Canada Geese
13. Pronghorns
14. King Salmon
15. Beavers
16. Snow Geese
17. Mule Deer
18. Bald Eagles
19. Bighorn Sheep
20. Gray Whales

DISCOVERING WILDLIFE

I spend a lot of time by myself, but I rarely feel alone. The company of animals is deeply satisfying, whether it's the steady presence of finches at the bird feeder or merely crossing paths with fresh deer tracks. Once you know a little bit about wildlife—where animals live, what they eat, what their missions are—there is always something to look for, something to see, something to think about. There is always company to keep.

Going Wild is more than a set of directions to viewing sites, it's an invitation to discover wildlife within the context of season and habitat. In each chapter, I describe a field trip (twenty in all, five for each season) centered around an admittedly subjective interpretation of what I find interesting about certain Pacific Northwest species. Travel-related information is included at the end of each chapter. If you can't make it to Oregon's farthest corner to watch pronghorns run, or to the Olympic Peninsula to listen to elk bugle, let me take you in these pages. If you can go, I hope what you read here will enhance your own experience.

The *Going Wild* trip list is idiosyncratic. Some of the destinations, such as Bowerman Basin for migrating shorebirds and Klamath Basin for wintering bald eagles, could be classified as definitive wildlife-viewing experiences. But most of the trips, including Mima Mounds for butterfly watching and the Lava Lands for bats, are simply productive wildlife-watching spots I have personally enjoyed. Public access and the impact of wildlife watchers were important considerations in selecting which destinations to include, so nearly every trip is to a refuge, park, or national forest where the land and the animals on it are at least minimally prepared for human presence. Use what you learn by reading and exploring to discover your own secret places.

You don't need to be a hard-core camper or hiker to go wild. Binoculars are the only special equipment you really should have. In most cases you can choose to camp or stay in a motel or lodge. No backpacking is required, although some trips are more challenging than others in terms of distance, road conditions, and lack of facilities.

Of the main trips, many require driving on at least some unpaved roads, but for every outing, two-wheel-drive and a little common sense will get you as far as you need to go. For the more remote trips, know your own limits and the limits of your vehicle. The same goes for traveling in winter. Weather and road conditions vary from season to season and year to year so call ahead for information. Always carry tools, a spare tire, water, DeLorme Mapping Company's Washington and Oregon atlases (available at many bookstores and sporting goods stores), and an emergency kit with flares and first aid supplies. In winter, also carry tire chains, a shovel, and blankets.

Basic routes to the field trip destinations are provided throughout, but these directions are not intended to be the sole means of finding your way. Follow the suggested route, or study your maps for interesting alternatives. Travel back roads when you can—the interstate and major highways may be efficient, but they isolate you from the land. It's hard to hear a meadowlark at sixty-five miles-per-hour, and you can't pull over on Interstate 5 to watch a red-tailed hawk catch a mouse.

Included with the travel-related information at the end of each chapter are suggestions of other places to see similar wildlife sights. I haven't been to every one of those sites myself, but all are reported to have the species of interest and appear to hold promise for adventure. Maybe I'll see you there.

Wherever you go and however you get there, please be gentle. Respect the animals, the land, other wildlife watchers, and laws of private property. You can kill wildlife by trying to get too close or by disturbing animals or habitat for a better photograph. Wild animals work within a tight energy budget, and unnecessary expenditures can make the difference between survival and death. Every season has its demands. In winter, animals must cope with harsh weather and reduced food supplies; spring presses wildlife with the demands of reproduction and, in some cases, migration. In the summer, adults are busy feeding young, and fall is the final chance to put on fat for the coming winter and perhaps for a second migration.

The choices you make affect wildlife. In the field, for instance, you can stay in your car to minimize disturbance to snow geese and resist the urge to collect tidepool creatures. At home, use recycled materials and conserve energy to reduce your impact on the environment we share with all living things.

It takes a little effort to meet your animal cohabitants on their home turf. And of course, effort does not guarantee success. It doesn't matter how early you get up, how far you drive, how badly you want to see something, or what someone else saw yesterday or five minutes ago. Sometimes you see what you came for, sometimes you don't. That's what makes it wildlife watching and not going to the zoo.

But don't give up. Be patient, quiet, and attentive. Go slow. Steal a wolf nap in a deer bed and wait for wildlife to come to you. Even if you don't see what you came for, you will see plants, other animals, colors, patterns, tracks, and—if you look closely—your own shadow and your own heart.

SPRING

CHAPTER 1

BASIN AND CRANE

Sandhill Cranes at Malheur National Wildlife Refuge, Oregon

From another world, higher than the clouds, faint sounds come clattering down like bamboo rain, conjured more than heard. The sound brightens into a commotion of voices as the sandhill cranes parachute down, drifting, spiraling, descending, until finally they are fifteen feet above the little pond. Voices now stilled, thirty great birds wheel tighter, circling once and once more, wind shushing under six-foot spans of wing. The cranes step from the air onto an alkaline crust at the edge of the pond and stop, motionless, time suspended. Gray statuary, quiet and serene. Elegant, aboriginal.

The world resumes its spin, and the birds melt back into life and transcend the eight steps to the water. They wade in, water murmuring around thin legs. One crane coughs quietly; several drink. They are the color of pewter with a blush of white on each cheek and a British redcoat-red crown. Eyes are bright tangerine.

These sandhill cranes will spend the night here in Malheur National Wildlife Refuge and in the morning will join other migrants to feed in farm fields nearby. Then one day in late spring they won't stop at the fields but will continue north until they reach familiar nesting grounds in Alaska. They will go the way they came—gracefully—circling back toward the clouds, cacophonous, until specks and sounds evaporate.

Near Oregon's southeastern corner, the Malheur refuge covers 184,000 not-on-the-way-to-anywhere acres of marshlands, meadows, shallow lakes, dry lake beds, big sagebrush, little sagebrush, rabbit brush, and bunchgrass. Driving down the south side of the ridge that separates the town of Burns from Malheur, the Malheur–Harney Basin looks like the tear-stained cheek of an old man. Shallow water moistens acres of scrubby ground and rivulets trace wrinkles in the red-brown earth. Malheur is at the northernmost reach of the Great Basin, a 200,000-square-mile area in which lakes and rivers have no outlet to the sea.

The largest freshwater marsh in the western United States, Malheur Lake is one of the most extensive wetland complexes in the whole of North America. Water levels can fluctuate radically from year to year, but the lake averages twenty miles long, twelve miles wide, and six feet or less deep.

In a remote land otherwise dominated by desert shrubs, stunted juniper, and volcanic dust, the wetlands are a wildlife magnet. Three major migration corridors within the Pacific Flyway converge here, creating a sort of giant collector and pump station for migrating cranes, waterfowl, shorebirds, songbirds, and birds of prey.

The Pacific, Central, Mississippi, and Atlantic flyways were designated in the late 1940s, when United States air space was divvied up for the purpose of managing migrating birds, primarily waterfowl and other game birds. A number of smaller migration corridors occur within each flyway. Even though certain species such as sandhill cranes and Canada geese occur in all four regions, populations within each are considered independently by the four flyway councils when making management recommendations. Bounded by the Pacific Ocean on the west, the eastern border of the Pacific Flyway follows the Continental Divide through Montana, Wyoming, Colorado, and New Mexico.

Of the six subspecies of sandhill crane, two—greater and lesser sandhills—can be seen at Malheur. The lesser sandhills, by far the most numerous of the two, merely stop over here on the way to Alaska. Most of the greater sandhill cranes, however, will go no farther. Lesser sandhills begin arriving in early March, and at the peak of migration in early April, as many as 12,000 may pass through the area. Most are gone by early May. Greater sandhills begin trickling into Malheur as early as February to claim or reclaim nesting territories. Between 180 and 200 pairs nest here and it's not unusual for the same pair to return to the same spot season after season. Young are present from mid-May to September.

Early spring is a magic time at Malheur. The presence of humans is minimal, and the air is pulled tight between the receding winter and building tension of spring. From the time I rolled down into the Malheur–Harney Basin, I crossed paths with other people only at a distance and didn't have to speak for two days. I got to the refuge at twilight and walked to the top of Coyote Butte to watch night pour over the land like Oregon's finest Pinot Noir. Meadowlarks, geese, and cranes called the darkness the rest of the way in. That night I dreamed I caught a pony and galloped bareback and bridleless across the sage plain.

In the morning, I scraped a thick layer of frost off the windshield and drove back toward Burns. It seemed odd to leave the refuge and drive to town to see wildlife, but the migrating lesser sandhills congregate to feed during the day in agricultural meadows around Burns. It was still before dawn when I got there, but cranes already filled the field across Highway 78 from the Harney County Veterinary Hospital. I pulled off the road and rolled down the window. A red-winged blackbird perched on the wire fence and kept me close company. He did all the talking.

Just beyond the wire, 200 cranes shared the field with hundreds of ducks, Canada geese, and about 2,000 snow geese—all calling and jostling. Avian whirlpools swirled up and down in a scene congested as an airport lobby on Easter weekend. Which, in a way, it was. The cranes were in the foreground, pecking, probing, vigorously ripping up clumps of dirt, looking for food. A cloud of more gregarious red-winged blackbirds surged around their feet like tidal foam, picking through the flotsam uprooted by the big birds. A green flatbed roared by, flushing the blackbirds in a whir of shocking bits of bright red. The cranes raised their heads in unison and watched the truck disappear. One, then another, then all looped their necks down to resume ripping. The blackbird tide swept back in. Cranes are among the most omnivorous of birds and will eat insects, seeds, grains, berries, worms, eggs, grass, lichen, frogs, mice, and aquatic plants and roots, depending on where they are and what time of year it is.

There were no great blue herons in the crowded field, but cranes and herons are often confused with one another. Both are about the same height, but cranes stand in a more soldierly posture, with necks held straighter. Cranes also hold their necks out straight in flight, while herons fold their necks back. When you see the two standing on the ground, the heron will look rather dressed up, with plumage frilling off its breast and head. The crane has a plainer look, except for its tail bustle, which is actually formed by folded-back wings. Cranes also have shorter beaks and smaller heads than herons, whose beaks are clearly spearlike. Flocking behavior is a dead giveaway—it's highly unusual to see herons gathered in a large group. The tall, small-headed laconic birds in Gary Larson's "Far Side" cartoons look to be crane caricatures.

As the morning traffic picked up, snow geese fell into the sky like a backward snow storm and headed for fields near the sewage ponds west of town. The cranes drifted to center field and continued to eat. I drifted my cold self into Burns for coffee.

Fossil evidence of cranes dates back at least 55 million years. Stylized adaptations of their leaping, twisting cotillion are reflected in the ceremonial dances of Australian aborigines, ancient Japanese Ainu, early Africans, and Native Americans.

Although we usually associate the crane's display with courtship, the dancing is an expression of general agitation and has been observed among cranes of all ages at all times of year.

The courtship ballet does, however, seem to inspire a particularly wild and abandoned performance. Male and female bow and curtsy. They leap like Baryshnikov and spin like Salome, prancing with wings caped, flinging bits of grass into the air. In pairs, the dance is theater. In a flock, it's Bourbon Street at Mardi Gras. The din can be heard a mile away. Early April mornings are the most promising times to catch Malheur's sandhills in performance.

Only a bird who can dance such a dance could have such a voice. The word *crane* comes from the Anglo-Saxon *cran,* meaning "to cry out." Chances are you will hear sandhills before you see them. Even from heights that render the birds invisible, the distinctive *karroook* announces their impending presence. The sound is part raven, part rattle, part riddle. I can't think of a crane without hearing its voice in my mind's ear. They call constantly during flight and are also likely to keep up a steady stream of vocalization while on the ground feeding.

Avian voice boxes are at the bottom of the windpipe instead of at the top, where mammals carry theirs. Special muscles can adjust membranal tension like a drum head. In cranes, as in swans, the windpipe forms a loop, adding to the vocal resonance. Convolutions lengthen into serpentine coils as the crane ages, and in old birds the windpipe may penetrate the breastbone. If you can't picture it, you can see similarly formed trumpeter swan windpipes in the tiny natural history museum at the Malheur refuge headquarters. I went there after I came down from Coyote Butte that first night, having read that the museum stayed open late. The headquarters compound was dark, but I found the museum building and tried the door. It was unlocked, so I let myself in and felt around for the light switch.

The fluorescent lights hummed and caught, and I was startled by the sudden reflection from 200 pairs of glass eyes. Cranes, geese, ducks, songbirds, shorebirds, and birds of prey stared from tall glass cases. In drawers below the cases, mice and other small mammals and eggs of all shapes, sizes, and colors were labeled and arrayed on padded beds. Wind whistled through cracks in the door, and dried leaves scraped loudly over the concrete walk outside; but no one came to break the spell of being alone in a museum on a dark night. I found the sandhill eggs, which were about three and a half inches long, and a muted brownish color

with darker dribbly spots. They looked huge next to the tiny, delicate, blue eggs of the ibis. In the privacy of this showing, the
room felt more like a spirit repository than a taxidermy display.
The mounts were in good condition, but were not of this decade.
The eggs, judging by the tags, had been taken in the 1940s to
1960s. One tag on a sandhill crane egg explained that it had been
taken because the collector presumed the egg to be infertile
because of its unusually large size.

Two of the world's fifteen crane species, the whooping and
sandhill crane, are found in North America. Whoopers are clinging to a thin thread of existence, but sandhill cranes can still be
counted in the hundreds of thousands. The largest numbers of
sandhill cranes are found in the Central Flyway. During spring
migration, these midcontinent sandhills gather in breathtaking
concentrations along the Platte River in Nebraska. The Pacific
population is much smaller, numbering about 20,000 to 25,000
birds. The lesser sandhill subspecies comprises about 90 percent of
the total sandhill population—a ratio that holds true both nation-
wide and in the Pacific population.

Most of the greater and lesser Pacific sandhill cranes that
migrate to and through Malheur spend the winter in California.
The majority of greaters winter about thirty miles south of
Sacramento; lessers winter near Stockton and south through the
Central Valley, especially near Merced.

Greater and lesser sandhill cranes are more different in their
habits than in their looks, although there are
slight distinctions in appearance. The
greater is larger; males weigh about
twelve pounds and are about four feet tall. Lessers are
just under four feet tall, weigh seven to eight pounds, and
may be a little darker gray. The foreheads of lesser sandhills
may also be slightly more pronounced than the foreheads
of greaters. In both subspecies, juveniles lack the red
cap and are more brownish in color. A good way to
tell greater from lesser is by circumstance. At Malheur,
if you see two sandhill cranes off by themselves away from con-
gregating flocks, they are probably nesting greaters. The lessers
tend to stay in groups and spend most of the day feeding.

In both sandhills, the redder the cap the older the bird. The white cheek patch also varies among individuals and is thought by some experts to display social status. Those experts who believe this assert that paired adults have bright white cheeks more often than adults who haven't as yet formed permanent bonds. The cheeks of unattached birds, the experts propose, are grayer. I tried to make a study of this but kept losing track of who was with whom among Malheur's milling crane crowds. Sandhills might indeed have tight family groups, but they also seem to be terrific mixers.

There may be a method to this mixing. Selecting the right mate appears to be far from haphazard. Cranes can spend three or four years trying out several prospective partners before finding the match that will endure. Even in the wild, sandhills have been known to live more than twenty-three years, so fidelity may offer a biological advantage. Familiar mates share knowledge and experience and have a proven history of reproductive success.

Both male and female are attentive parents. Together, they build a ground nest of grasses or reeds several inches thick and several feet wide. They also share responsibility for incubating eggs and rearing offspring. The female typically lays two eggs, but often only one survives. Young cranes, like white pelicans and some other species of birds, are thought to practice "obligate siblicide," in which one nestling kills any others before leaving the nest, even in times of plenty. The precocious young crane can walk almost immediately upon hatching and is soon able to catch insects. Still, parents continue to feed the chick for up to six months, and the young bird stays with its parents until the following spring, when breeding season begins again.

Long life spans, low reproductive rates, and the inability to adapt easily to environmental change make sandhills vulnerable to modern pressures. The biggest threat is loss of habitat. Sandhills like to roost at night standing in the water, but suitable shallow wetlands are being drained and developed at warp speed. Flocks are forced to condense unnaturally into smaller and smaller areas. Predation on nests by ravens and coyotes stresses populations, and illegal shootings and legal hunting seasons also take a toll. Hunting for sandhill cranes is allowed in most of the states within the Central Flyway and, although neither Washington nor Oregon permits the hunting of sandhill cranes, limited seasons are being introduced into some states within the Pacific Flyway.

Generally speaking, sandhill cranes are in pretty good shape, but we should be careful not to take their presence for granted. Lying in an open field in the Malheur Basin, I watched a hundred or so sandhills relax to earth. It struck me that maybe the reason I had been dreaming so richly here was because every night the cranes carried down dream packages, tied to their backs like Zuni fetishes. In any case, the flight and voice of a sandhill crane surely kindles contemplation. Maybe the cranes will take my meditations with them when they go, circling back into the atmosphere to carry the journey, and my daydreams, northward.

Timing Your Visit: The migration of lesser sandhill cranes through Malheur National Wildlife Refuge peaks in early April.

Contact: For more information on Malheur National Wildlife Refuge, contact refuge headquarters, HC-72 Box 245, Princeton, OR 97721; (503)493-2612.

Getting There: To get to Malheur from Bend, take Highway 20 east 130 miles to Burns, and then take Highway 205 south. In about 25 miles, look for the refuge sign and turn east on the county road toward Princeton. Refuge headquarters is ahead about 9 miles.

Accommodations: For information on area facilities, contact the Harney County Chamber of Commerce, 18 West D Street, Burns, OR 97720; (503)573-2636.

WHERE ELSE TO SEE SANDHILL CRANES

WASHINGTON
Ridgefield National Wildlife Refuge, southwestern Washington: Spring finds sandhill cranes and other migrants at this refuge of farmland, marshes, ponds, and pastures bordering the Columbia River. Many opportunities exist for walking through this refuge.

To get to Ridgefield from Vancouver, Washington, take I-5 north to the Ridgefield exit. Go west 3 miles to Ridgefield; refuge headquarters is at 210 N. Main Street.

For more information on Ridgefield National Wildlife Refuge, contact refuge headquarters, 210 N. Main Street, Ridgefield, WA 98642; (206)887-4071. For information on area facilities, contact the Vancouver–Clark County Visitor Bureau, 404 E. 15th Street, Suite 11, Vancouver, WA 98663; (206)693-1313.

Mansfield area, central Washington: There is no wildlife refuge here, but there are miles and miles of cultivated land where cranes feed during their migration. Work the square blocks of roads between Mansfield and Sims Corner to the east at the junction of State Routes 172 and 17. Keep an eye on the sky and stop periodically to listen. At dawn and dusk, watch for flocks rising and descending.

To get to Mansfield from Wenatchee, take Highway 2 east and then turn north on State Route 172 and follow it to Mansfield.

For information on area facilities, contact the Grand Coulee Dam Area Chamber of Commerce, P.O. Box 760, Grand Coulee, WA 99133; (509)633-3074.

OREGON

Ladd Marsh Wildlife Area, northeastern Oregon: Sandhill cranes can be found near La Grande in this refuge, which is part farmland and part marsh. Passage within the wildlife area is controlled, so check with the Oregon Department of Fish and Wildlife for current access information.

To get to Ladd Marsh from La Grande, take I-84 south to exit 268. Viewpoints are off the Foothill–Ladd Canyon Road.

For more information on Ladd Marsh, contact the Oregon Department of Fish and Wildlife, Box 339, La Grande, OR 97850; (503)963-2138. For information on area facilities, contact the La Grande–Union County Chamber of Commerce, 1502 N. Pine, La Grande, OR 97850; (503)963-8588.

Summer Lake Wildlife Area, south-central Oregon: This desert wetland is a major rest stop for migrating birds, including lesser sandhill cranes and snow geese.

To get to Summer Lake from Bend, take Highway 97 south through LaPine. Just past LaPine, turn east on Highway 31 to Summer Lake.

For more information on Summer Lake Wildlife Area, contact the Oregon Department of Fish and Wildlife, Box 8, Hines, OR 97738; (503)573-6582. For information on area facilities, contact the Lake County Chamber of Commerce, Lakeview, OR 97630-1577; (503)947-6040.

CHAPTER 2

COMMUNITY RELATIONS
A Wildlife Sampler at Stehekin, Washington

Yesterday, someone saw a cougar standing on the road. There were nine sightings last year. This morning, it was a black bear, just a little way up from High Bridge. Last week it was a four-point elk; last spring, a moose.

Since there's only one road in Stehekin, everybody uses it at one time or another, be they cougar, bear, elk, moose, deer, or human. And since you can't drive to the little settlement at the north end of central Washington's Lake Chelan, the ratio of cars to critters is pretty fair. The twenty-three-mile Stehekin Road starts at the dock and ends a few miles short of Cascade Pass in

North Cascades National Park. Internally combusted traffic on the road is limited to a few shuttle vehicles and a smattering of mostly old cars and trucks barged in by the small group of permanent, people-type residents.

You can get to Stehekin by boat, small plane, or on foot over the mountains from various points along the North Cascades Highway (Highway 20) or Twisp River Road. Once you're there, the last thing on your mind will be getting back out.

The diversity of wildlife is what makes this place special, not one single species; so call this trip the Stehekin Surprise and explore different wildlife communities within the greater North Cascades ecosystem to see what you can find. Try the forest community for bears eating berries, grouse eating grasshoppers, and porcupines doing whatever they want; or get into the high-country community, where mountain goats and marmots stand watch among the ground-hugging heathers. Visit the river community, where beavers go about their chores while trout hide in the shade of downed trees. And, of course, don't forget the Stehekin community, where people bake cinnamon rolls and drive shuttles and have children who pretend they're butterflies in school plays.

The most popular way of getting to Stehekin is by passenger ferry from the town of Chelan or from Field's Point. Two commercial vessels ply the fifty-mile route—the 350-passenger *Lady of the Lake II* and the faster, 150-passenger *Lady Express*. Lake Chelan has not been without a *Lady* since 1900, when the Stehekin area was already firmly abuzz with miners, prospectors, and homesteaders.

The four-hour ride up the long, narrow lake on the *Lady II* is like a child's-plate version of the trip up the Inside Passage to Alaska. (The *Lady Express* makes the uplake trip in two hours and fifteen minutes.) Distances are more moderate, the forest isn't as dense, and, of course, there are no killer whales, but the fifty-mile-long lake is possessed of a similar fjordlike essence. The longest natural lake in Washington and third-deepest lake in the United States, Lake Chelan fills the base of a U-shaped, glacially carved trough that averages about a mile wide throughout most of its entire length.

Peering over the rail into the dark water, I'm sure the bottom must be way down there even before the boat's loudspeaker announces the lake to be 1,500 feet at its deepest point. If you were to stand on the bottom, you would be almost 400 feet below sea level; then if you shot straight up to intersect an imaginary line drawn out from adjacent Pyramid Peak, you would have just rocketed the deepest gorge in the country—deeper than the Grand Canyon and Hell's Canyon, which only look deeper because they're not filled with more than a quarter-mile of water.

Town sinks quickly into the frothy stern wake, and the shoreline loses its sprawl of cabins and condos when the road gives out about twenty miles uplake. Only the south end of Lake Chelan is developed because the rest of the lake is packed in all the way around by the Wenatchee National Forest, Glacier Peak Wilderness, North Cascades National Park, Lake Chelan National Recreation Area, Lake Chelan–Sawtooth Wilderness, and Okanogan National Forest.

The *Lady* slips past steep, forest-stubbled hillsides that fall right into the water. In places along the shore, the rocky land exposes its pressed layers to help you feel how heavily the crust of the earth rides.

I watch the hillsides for mountain goats and discover a knack for spotting white rocks. About halfway up the lake on the northeast side, the area between Safety Harbor Creek and Prince Creek is an important mountain goat wintering area. June is a little late in the season for viewing goats from the boat, but you never know; so I keep looking. It's hard to find an easier, more pleasant way to observe mountain goats in their natural habitat. You can be eating a sandwich one minute and looking at a goat the next. No sweat.

Mountain goats are native to the Cascades. The problem goats you may have heard about are in the Olympic Mountains, where goats aren't native but were introduced before Olympic National Park was established. Park officials fear the goats are destroying fragile alpine habitat and so are removing the Olympic Park goats. Introduced species often survive in a new environment by outcompeting native residents. Native plants or animals may be wiped out completely, or at the very least, the original balance of a community is upset.

But mountain goats are ecosystem insiders here in the

Cascades. One of their contributions to the early community was providing the Tsill-ane people, who lived by the south end of Lake Chelan, with meat and trade goods. The Tsill-anes (meaning "deep notch" or "deep water") would canoe to the head of the lake and then make their way over Cascade Pass to trade with the Skagit people. Goat wool was exchanged for dried clams, salmon, and seashells.

After white settlers arrived in force in the 1800s, the Tsill-ane, whose name came to be called "Chelan," were pushed onto a reservation that stretched from the north shore of the lake to the Canadian border. Lacking a broader sense of community, the white settlers eventually decided to take that land too, and the Columbia Reservation treaty was nullified by Congress in 1886.

I didn't see a goat or a bear before we docked at Stehekin, but if any of my rocks or shadows had turned into either, the captain would have slowed down and approached the shore for better views and picture taking. The *Lady* likes to watch wildlife.

Depending on whether your glass is half empty or half full, Stehekin is the end of the line or the beginning of it. There are no phones there, no television, limited accommodations, and a shuttle service that runs on its own schedule, not yours. But looked at the other way, there are thousands of acres of wilderness, hundreds of miles of trails, hours of quiet, ready solitude, and a prosperity of wildlife lost from most other parts of the Northwest.

If you're taking the boat back out the same day, you'll have time to ride the special blue school bus to Rainbow Falls and back, or walk the Imus Nature Trail, or check out the historical features of Stehekin, or attend a Park Service program. If you're taking the boat back out the same day, you'll be sorry.

If you're staying, you have about an hour and a half from the time the boat docks until the afternoon shuttle van leaves Stehekin. Some of the private lodging facilities offer transportation, but if you're camping or staying at the North Cascades Lodge, which is located right at the boat landing, the shuttle is your ticket to ride. The fourteen-passenger van makes the twenty-two-mile round trip from Stehekin Landing up the road to High Bridge and back twice a day. Arrangements can easily be made to ride the shuttle past High Bridge. Numerous trails take off from the Stehekin Road, and the shuttle will let you off wherever you want. There's plenty of time to get oriented at the ranger station and to buy supplies at one of the several little stores. Don't miss the bakery just up the road. Permits are required for overnight backcountry camping. Campsites can be reserved and the free permits obtained in advance, or you can take a chance and sign up when you get there.

Big Dave was the ranger on duty at the Golden West Visitor Center when I got there. Or maybe it's Tall Dave. Maybe it's Big Tall Dave. Anyway, he sold me Green Trail maps and put so much thought and enthusiasm into helping me plan my hikes that I thought maybe he was coming along. Another ranger, Karen, appeared at the desk and joined the conference. As her current specialty was animal tracks and sign, she carefully rated each suggested trail according to the scat factor. I thought maybe now I had two hiking companions. Karen was on the two o'clock shuttle when it left Stehekin but only went as far as her cabin. A different ranger, Curt, was at the wheel.

If there's a driveway to heaven, it's probably a lot like the Stehekin Road. The mostly one-lane, mostly gravel road follows the Stehekin River as it climbs up the valley. Along the route, sunlight trickles through red and yellow cedar, Douglas fir, ponderosa pine, white pine, hemlock, broadleaf maple, and Pacific dogwood. Even though the Chelan drainage is on the eastern side of the Cascades, moisture-loving flora of the western side can also survive here, creating a unique diversity of plant species.

Curt pulled over and reached out the window to hang a handmade fabric bag on a nail pounded into a tree. The Stehekin mail service. He hung bags at three different trees before we made the scheduled stop at Rainbow Falls. The 312-foot falls plunge down in a fury of mist and roar. I hear Big Tall Dave climbed it one winter when it was froze hard.

Like the *Lady*, the shuttle van is never in such a hurry that it can't stop to admire something. If I pointed at a flower, we would stop for a better look. Curt knew a little something of just about everything, and we stopped for mule deer, Columbia tiger lilies, flowering dogwoods, a beaver-chewed tree, and a western yew. Standing by a tree during the scheduled High Bridge stop, I held out my hand and a wood nymph landed on it. The pumpkin pie-colored butterfly rested for a while before it began to tap its tongue against my sweaty arm.

It seemed funny to make the several scheduled stopovers when I was the only rider and we were in the middle of nowhere, but I guess you never know when someone might just walk out of the woods and expect the bus to be there. We left High Bridge at three o'clock, right on time.

I asked to be let out at the first wagon-wheel trail, about a mile and a quarter farther along. Even before I told him, Curt knew I must be going to Coon Lake. The moderately easy, two-and-a-half-mile trail pushes away from the road, skirts Coon Lake, and then hooks back up with the road at High Bridge. He let me off and steered the van back south.

Along the trail, afternoon heat pulled and mixed fragrances from flowering shrubs, trail dust, and pine needles. Chaste-looking white bead lilies shone alongside the trail like young girls at first communion.

I invited myself to a late lunch at what I took to be the Coon Lake community center, a flat rock near the water, busied by ants. A seven-inch western fence lizard (member of the iguana family) scurried by, pausing to do a few push-ups and flash me some blue. Rattlesnakes live in this area too. Theoretically they don't bite unless provoked, but some trail guides suggest not letting kids be first down the path.

Coon Lake is really a marshy pond. As I settled down, two goldeneye ducks dashed across the water in exaggerated panic. They flurried and squawked and churned longer than they needed to, so I began to think I wasn't the problem. I moved from the rock to a log—not caring to be one with the ants—and opened my orange juice. The ducks settled down, and when they pad-dled back seven tiny ducklings came beating out of the marsh grass like drowning bumblebees.

Bright blue damselflies—slim-bodied dragon-flies—skimmed the water, hunting tiny insects that hovered over the surface. Birds and frogs, two vocal and visible Coon Lake residents, find damselflies delectable.

damsel fly

Woods pushed in close around the pond. Wind swished through the canopy high overhead, but the air was still around my shoulders. A muskrat climbed out of the water, chewed down some brush, and towed a leafy mouthful back across the pool. Muskrats keep the cattails and rushes clipped back so that there's plenty of open water for duck families.

The bus wasn't at High Bridge when I got there, so to pass the time, I wandered down the Agnes Creek Trail, which takes off from the other side of the road. About a mile down the narrow path, something started crashing in the bushes fifty yards away. *Crack! Rustle rustle rustle. Crack!* I tried looking into the dense vegetation but saw only a black shadow. *Crack!*

My adrenaline system was convinced it was a bear. But my brain wasn't sure; so my feet stepped to the edge of the trail and my mouth said, "Hello?"

RUSTLE RUSTLE RUSTLE RUSTLE.

Suddenly unified, brain, feet, and mouth turned tail and beat it back to the road, not needing to know what was making the commotion. Curt was waiting. He and Steve, another ranger just back from a hike, were discussing how to go about looking for me if I didn't show up. A community of strangers. On the way back to Stehekin we picked up Karen. She had lipstick on and was going to a potluck. A community of friends.

The next day, Karen was at the wheel of the morning shuttle. It was just the two of us and we stopped for cinnamon rolls and a western tanager. I had originally planned on walking the Stehekin River Trail (good for scat, beavers, and harlequin ducks) and then catching the afternoon *Lady II* back to Chelan. But I changed my mind and made reservations on the evening floatplane so I could go with Steve to try to reach what looks like an old mine shaft visible from Bridge Creek Camp. He flagged us down from the road near his cabin and we drove on to Bridge Creek, about five miles past High Bridge.

We approached the mine from the Goode Ridge Trail—a steep stack of switchbacks that gains about 4,400 feet in five miles. Steve, who was giving an evening program on mining, pushed me up the switchbacks with silly jokes and Stehekin mining stories. Seems the first major ore discovery in the area was in 1886. Let me check my notes, but wasn't that the year Congress annulled the Columbia Reservation treaty? Although the ore wasn't high grade, it did contain amounts of gold, silver, and lead. The

Stehekin Road was built to supply the resultant crop of mines, which carried names like Black Warrior and Blue Devil. Most mining activity in the area had ceased by the late 1950s.

A blue grouse flushed from right beside the trail in the middle of a story. It flew up to a low limb and stared. Grouse may be responsible for more heart attacks on the trail than elevation gain. We had been listening to its *whup whup whup whup whup* all along, but were still caught by surprise.

We never found the mine, but the astonishing panorama from high on Goode Ridge was a view for God's building inspector.

Curt was waiting in the shuttle van when we came down. Ten minutes or so before our scheduled departure time, two people emerged unexpectedly from the woods to catch the bus. These folks, who in some other community would be called senior citizens, had walked over the mountains from the North Cascades Highway to get there.

The bus was full and everyone was going to Stehekin, but Curt honored each stop for the allotted layover. If other people had shown up from the woods, we would have found a place for them. I was late for the plane, but not by much, and got to sit in the copilot's seat. On the way back, we flew as high over the water as the water was deep. I felt light, and balanced, and like my community was a little bit larger than it had been just a week earlier.

Timing Your Visit: Spring is a dependable time to see a variety of wildlife near Stehekin. Mountain goats are most often seen from the *Lady* during the winter and early spring.

Contact: For more information on the Stehekin area, contact the U.S. Forest Service/National Park Service, Chelan Ranger District, P.O. Box 189, Chelan, WA 98816; (509)682-2576. For *Lady* information, contact the Lake Chelan Boat Company, P.O. Box 186, Chelan, WA 98816; (509)682-2224. For floatplane information, contact Chelan Airways, P.O. Box W, Chelan, WA 98816; (509)682-5555.

Getting There: To get to the Chelan dock for *Lady of the Lake II* and *Lady Express* from Wenatchee, take Highway 97 north 37 miles through Entiat to Chelan. To get to the Field's Point landing dock west of Chelan, take Highway 97 from Wenatchee, but turn left at Navarre Coulee Road, just past Winesap. At South Lakeshore Road, turn left and go about 13 miles.

Accommodations: For a list of public and private Stehekin facilities, contact the National Park Service, P.O. Box 7, Stehekin, WA 98852; the Chelan phone contact number is (509)682-2549. For information on Chelan area facilities, contact the Lake Chelan Chamber of Commerce, P.O. Box 216, Chelan, WA 98816; (509)682-2022.

WHERE ELSE TO SAMPLE WILDLIFE COMMUNITIES

WASHINGTON
Salmo Priest Wilderness Area, northeastern Washington: Grizzly bears, woodland caribou, gray wolves, elk, bats, rubber boas, and rattlesnakes have all been sighted here.

To get to Salmo Priest Wilderness Area from Spokane, take Highway 2 north and then Highway 211 north to Usk. Continue north on Highway 20. Just south of Ione, take Sullivan Lake Road northeast to Sullivan Lake; roads and trails to Salmo Priest are accessible from there.

For more information and maps of the Salmo Priest Wilderness Area, contact the Colville National Forest, Federal Building, Colville, WA 99114; (509)684-4557. For information on area facilities, contact the Ione Chamber of Commerce, P.O. Box 518, Ione, WA 99139; (509)442-3737.

Indian Heaven Wilderness area, southwestern Washington: This wilderness area in the Gifford Pinchot National Forest shelters a wide variety of plants and animals. Huckleberry fields cleared in the forest have enduring cultural and historical significance to Native Americans.

To get to Indian Heaven Wilderness Area from Vancouver, Washington, take Highway 14 east to Cook and turn north on Cook-Underwood Road. The road becomes South Prairie Road (Forest Road 66). From that point, use a Forest Service map to find your way to trails.

For more information on Indian Heaven Wilderness Area or

on area berry picking, contact the Forest Supervisor, Gifford Pinchot National Forest, 500 W. 12th Street, Vancouver, WA 98660; (206)696-7500. For information on area facilities, contact the Skamania County Chamber of Commerce, P.O. Box 1037G, Stevenson, WA 98648; (509)427-8911.

OREGON

Badger Creek Wilderness Area, northwestern Oregon: This habitat transition zone, featuring ponderosa pine, Oregon white oak, and sagebrush, draws a variety of wildlife.

To get to the Badger Creek Wilderness Area from Portland, take Highway 26 to Highway 35 (the Mount Hood Highway). Take Highway 35 to Forest Road 44 and follow F.R. 44 north and then east. Badger Creek is south of the road; use a good forest map to explore.

For more information on Badger Creek Wilderness Area, contact the Mount Hood National Forest, 19559 S.E. Division Street, Gresham, OR 97030; (503)667-0511. For information on area facilities, contact the Hood River County Chamber of Commerce, Port Marina Park, Hood River, OR 97031; (503)386-2000.

Three Sisters Wilderness Area, central Oregon: Douglas fir and pine forests and alpine meadows are home to wolverines, cougars, mink, trout, hummingbirds, and bald eagles.

To get to Three Sisters from Eugene, take Highway 126 east. A short way after the McKenzie Bridge, look for Highway 242. Take Highway 242 east. The Three Sisters Wilderness Area lies south of Highways 126 and 242. Use a forest map to find your way.

For more information on Three Sisters Wilderness Area, contact the Willamette National Forest, 210 E. 11th Avenue, Eugene, OR 97401; (503)687-6521. For information on area facilities, contact the Sisters Chamber of Commerce, P.O. Box 476, Sisters, OR 97759; (503)549-0251.

CHAPTER 3

FEATHERED BEDOUINS
Shorebirds at Bowerman Basin, Washington

Spring brings a restlessness of spirit almost too intense to bear. For some creatures, the only relief is to *go*. To walk, crawl, swim, fly *away*. Millions of birds, mammals, even insects are driven by a biological directive to get it in gear and go someplace safe and bountiful to introduce the next generation.

Bowerman Basin, a portion of Grays Harbor National Wildlife Refuge near Hoquiam, Washington, supports one of the most impressive spectacles of this primal obedience on the entire West Coast. Most days of the year, Bowerman Basin is a quiet and unassuming tidal mudflat on the north shore of Grays Harbor. Then one day in late April—*bam!*—it's center stage for 250,000 pacing, probing, peeping shorebirds. The day after that, the tally may be 500,000.

For two weeks, flocks roll in, fatten up at Bowerman Basin, and roll out to make room for the next wave. Before it's over, up to a million shorebirds may have feasted on the mudflat's notable affluence of worms, snails, and other edible invertebrates. Then one day they'll be gone as suddenly as they came.

Tides—high ones—are the key to shorebird viewing here. Bowerman Basin is the last place in Grays Harbor to flood at high tide and the first place exposed when the tide recedes. This gives birds the maximum amount of time to feed in the rich mud. The first year I went to Bowerman Basin to see the migratory horde, I thought I was being very smart to arrange my trip around the lowest tide. I got up in the middle of the night, drove two and a half hours, and was at Grays Harbor precisely at low tide, right before the sun came up. The more mudflat exposed to the hungry birds the better, I reasoned. Good thought, bad idea. The place looked abandoned. Nearly all 400,000 of the birds I knew to be there had followed the receding water and were feeding far out on the flats. I could have been looking at eraser dust. High tide, of course, pushes the shorebirds together and up into the basin where you can see them. Particularly high tides push the mass of birds to within about twenty feet of viewing areas—so close that their restlessness is contagious.

When I told a U.S. Fish and Wildlife Service biologist about my embarrassing error in judgment, all he said was, "Well, at least you had a plan." Some people, it seems, time their visits to correspond with the end of Sunday lunch, which doesn't qualify as a plan since it doesn't include consideration of the tides. Other people time their visits around the calendar, which also doesn't qualify because birds can't read and are known to be late or early. Call the refuge, check the tide book, make a plan.

Bowerman Basin is the farthest north of four shorebird "staging areas" on the West Coast of the continental United States. Staging areas are sites where migrating birds traditionally collect and feed during migration. The other important shorebird staging areas in the Lower 48 are Humboldt and San Francisco bays in California and Washington's Willapa Bay. After Bowerman Basin, most birds don't stop again until they reach the Copper River Delta in Alaska, although some may pause at the Fraser River Delta in Canada and the Stikine River Delta in Southeast Alaska. Once in Alaska, the shorebirds fan out all along Alaska's north and west coasts to nest.

Eighty-five to ninety-five percent of the migrants you'll see at Bowerman Basin are sparrow-sized western sandpipers. These tiny birds fly from Argentina to Alaska, mostly at night, and almost in orbit it seems, sometimes two miles high. The very thought of it worries me to death.

Shorebirds only stage like this on their northward migration in the spring, so don't wait for the return engagement. The southward trip is more leisurely, with individual birds leaving for wintering areas in North, Central, and South America anytime from June through October.

The term *shorebird* is a catchall phrase for small birds that wade but don't swim. Just about any shore will do, too—shorebirds are found around inland lakes and wetlands as well as at ocean beaches. In the western states alone, there are sixty species of sandpiper and sandpiperlike birds, a dozen plovers, and a bridge mix of others, including oystercatchers, avocets, stilts, snipes, curlews, and phalaropes (the one exception to the no-swimming rule).

On the way into Bowerman Basin this year—a half-hour before *high* tide—I noticed a peregrine falcon sitting on a gnarl of driftwood, preening. Peregrines follow the shorebird migration, snacking their way north on downy hors d'oeuvres.

Ignoring the peregrine, a merlin streaked by and strafed the feeding mass, peeling a thousand sandpipers off the mud into a tight-formation flight team. What on the ground was a flock of little, brown birds with white bellies became, in the air, a silvery school of tropical fish. Evading the small falcon, the flock veered, twisted, flashed white, twisted around on itself, flashed brown, and fell back to earth. The shorebirds are here to eat; these death-defying aerobatics are a distraction, so the flock wastes as little time as possible with the falcon.

If shorebirds had a slogan, it would be "Fat Power." Gaining and using fat reserves efficiently is central to their success. Fat accumulated from the Bowerman Basin binge can comfortably fuel the birds the remaining 1,500 miles to Alaska. Gram for gram, fat is said to contain nearly as much energy as gasoline, twice the energy of protein, and eight times more potential energy than stored carbohydrates. This high-octane fuel powers a bird's specialized respiratory and muscular systems, resulting in one efficient little flying unit. Many of the other smaller species of birds are equally energy-efficient. It has been reported in at least one scientific journal that if a blackpoll warbler burned gas it would get 720,000 miles per gallon. I couldn't find the supporting calculations but can't resist repeating the assertion.

In addition to a bird's conventional lungs, supplementary air sacs branch out into their hollow bones, boosting oxygen exchange and regulating internal temperatures. Birds have the highest operating temperatures of all animals, averaging about 110 degrees Fahrenheit. Biologists estimate that a pigeon, for example, uses about one-quarter of its air intake for breathing and three-quarters for cooling.

It has always been clear in the metaphorical sense that birds have great heart, and physiology bears this out. The proportion of heart to body weight in birds is three to six times what it is in humans.

Our fascination with birds and their habits predates the Audubon Society by centuries. Aristotle recorded his personal thoughts and observations on migration 2,300 years ago. Some of his ideas were right on, some were way out, and both persisted for two millennia. He was the first to note vertical migration—in which birds change elevations with the season—but he also believed in transmutation, an alchemical sort of idea that had redstarts turning into robins in the winter.

Other hypotheses developed over time. In 1703, a "Person of Learning and Piety" wrote "An Essay toward the Probable Solution of this Question: Whence come the Stork and the Turtledove, the Crane, and the Swallow, when they Know and Observe the Appointed Time of their Coming." The probable solution declared therein was that birds flew to the moon. Maybe the writer had been sitting in his garden on a spring night and noticed silhouettes of migrating birds passing before the full moon. The sight can still inspire wonder, if perhaps not piety.

Although we now know quite a bit about where birds go,

scientists still aren't certain what triggers migration and how birds find their way. Photoperiodism (reactions to changing hours of daylight), weather, hormones, and availability of food are all possible cues for beginning the migration; and the moon, stars, landmarks, the sun's angle, and the earth's magnetic field have all been investigated for their roles in avian navigation.

The quarter-million birds tattooing the mud in Bowerman Basin weren't spilling any secrets, but I did learn from other bird watchers that most of the birds had just come nonstop from San Francisco Bay. I also heard that biologists had traced the radio-tagged body of one hapless sandpiper to the burrow of a Bay Area ground squirrel. The Fish and Wildlife Service volunteer relating the story nervously shifted her handheld antenna and twisted the receiver dial for five other frequencies. Maybe the tagged birds she was listening for had simply taken a time-out in an unknown rest stop along the way. Yeah, I'm sure that's what must have happened.

As the tide ebbed, the shorebirds got excited and flung themselves out over the exposing mud. The 40,000 dunlin who winter in Grays Harbor must have wondered what hit them. A gentle hiss rose from the feeding crowd as a multitude of bills probed for food. The shorebirds primarily feed on Bowerman Basin's ample supply of amphipods (small sandhopperlike crustaceans), but also eat other tiny crustaceans, clams, and marine worms. Flocks shifted around, flying low to the ground like dust blowing along a road.

Because of the varying lengths and shapes of shorebird bills, different species can work the mud right next to each other and not be in competition for food—neighborliness through niche. (In natural science, the term *niche* refers to an animal's ecological role or place within the food web, not to the rock or cave or hemisphere where it lives. A niche for everything, and everything in its niche. Nature can be so tidy when it wants to be.) Each type of shorebird bill—long, short, upturned, downturned, straight, or somewhere in between—is designed to exploit a different layer of mud so there's usually plenty of food for everybody. Distributed down through the substrate are such invertebrates as insects and their larvae, tiny crustaceans (types of shrimp, crabs, barnacles, and sand fleas), small mollusks (various snails, clams, and mussels), and marine worms.

In terms of pure biomass, mudflats are among the richest ecosystems in the world. There are as many invertebrate organisms in one square yard of Bowerman Basin mud as there are people in Grays Harbor County.

With its springtime shorebird abundance and diversity, Bowerman Basin is a great place to learn your pipers from your plovers. Two dozen species, ranging in size from the five-inch least sandpiper to the eighteen-inch whimbrel, commonly use the harbor. Western sandpipers are by far most abundant, then dunlins, followed by dowitchers, semipalmated plovers, and least sandpipers. Pull up a log, prop open your bird book, and focus on the details.

If it's six or seven inches tall with a brown back, white belly, and rust-colored cap, and is obviously in the majority, it's a western sandpiper. Right from your driftwood davenport you may be looking at a significant portion of the entire western sandpiper population. Thinking about this makes me as nervous as thinking about their high night flights. Right around Christmas of 1988, storms pushed a slick of oil from a major spill off the coast into Grays Harbor. Fortunately, not much oil drifted into Bowerman Basin, but if it had, the heavy crude could have suffocated the organisms living in the mud, making that *three* staging areas on the entire West Coast. What if the spill had occurred in late April?

Sandpipers are brownish birds with white bellies and generally walk along the shore methodically probing the mud. If it's not a western but it is a sandpiper, it could be one of seven sandpipers that are found in Grays Harbor. Birders lump the three smallest species—western, least, and semipalmated—together as "peeps."

Dunlins are somewhat larger than western sandpipers and have slightly drooping bills. In the spring, dunlins sport black belly patches. Looking hunched over and neckless, they peck furiously at the mud, run a short distance, peck and run, peck and run.

Dowitchers are one of the more common large shorebirds you'll see. The ten- to twelve-inch-tall birds probe the mud in a sewing machine motion with their two-and-a-half- to three-inch-long bills. In the spring they may have rust-colored bellies.

Semipalmated plovers are also fairly common. With their

partially webbed (semipalmated) feet, these seven-inch-tall birds skip easily over the soft mud to feed on surface organisms. As a group, plovers are built more compactly than sandpipers, and have thick necks and pigeonlike eyes. Nearly all of them, including the familiar killdeer, share the run-stop-look habit.

If it swims, it's a phalarope. Phalaropes like to spin around in the water like tops, stirring up food from the bottom.

Watching birds at Bowerman Basin is an excellent viewing opportunity, but it is not what you'd call a wilderness experience. The log yard and smoking stacks of the Hoquiam lumber mill dominate the scenery on the way in. After you park, you walk (quite probably behind someone else) past a small airfield to get to the trail leading to viewing areas. "Trail" is always in quotes in the U.S. Fish and Wildlife Service brochures: the path skirting the mudflat out to the end of the spit is simply a track beaten down in four-foot-tall marsh grass. Occasionally, the track disappears under five inches of black muck. It's dependably muddy. Take knee-high boots and always be prepared for rain.

But save some appreciation for the surrounding country, which is haunting, and crushingly beautiful in the places where dark forests and free-flowing rivers still court black-tailed deer, coyotes, osprey, great blue herons, steelhead, and salmon.

Stepping off the road onto the "trail," I had mud splattered up to my hip pockets before I could say semipalmated plover. Slogging along, I passed a marsh wren perched nearly at eye level in the tall, stiff grass. As it sang me past, I looked straight down its pink throat. Crossing the shorter salt grass, I reached the tip of the spit, where the beach firms up. Old pilings snaggled across the mouth of the basin like bad teeth; dunlins dashed back and forth across the foamy lip of the receding tide.

In 1988 (before the spill), the U.S. Congress authorized the establishment of a National Wildlife Refuge at Bowerman Basin. As of 1992, the U.S. Fish and Wildlife Service had purchased 68 acres from the City of Hoquiam, and was negotiating with the Port of Grays Harbor for an additional 1,400 acres of marsh and mudflat. Development of the refuge (a visitors' center, habitat restoration, boardwalks, interpretive signs, and other enhancements) is awaiting more funds and the subsequent acquisition of land. For now, the Port is graciously allowing access to the public.

Thousands of acres of Grays Harbor have already been filled in. Bowerman Field Airport, including the lot you park in and the road you walk on, rests on dredged sediments that were piled on the tideland. No end of stuff to worry about.

The feeding shorebirds had sorted themselves out as the tide ebbed: least sandpipers staying high on the exposed mud, westerns and dunlins fanning out lower, dowitchers keeping their feet wet. Late-morning sun coaxed rich, briny smells out of the mud.

The peregrine circled high, looking for some fast food. A cold front was moving in from the north, and ground squirrels were on the loose in San Francisco. A knot of western sandpipers, looking entirely too vulnerable, peeped and whistled at the water's edge. I'd like to put all 250,000 of them on a bus.

Timing Your Visit: Peak numbers of migrating shorebirds are in Bowerman Basin in mid- to late April. Best viewing is one hour before to one hour after high tide. The higher the tide, the better.

Contact: For information on visiting Grays Harbor National Wildlife Refuge, contact the Nisqually National Wildlife Refuge, 100 Brown Farm Road, Olympia, WA 98506; (206)753-9467. Refuge staff can tell you whether the birds have arrived in the basin. They also usually know the times for high and low tides.

Getting There: To get to Grays Harbor National Wildlife Refuge from Aberdeen, take U.S. Highway 101 north through neighboring Hoquiam and then take Highway 109 toward Ocean Shores. In a mile or so, turn left on Paulson Road into the airport. Turn right on Airport Way.

Accommodations: For information on area facilities, contact the Grays Harbor Chamber of Commerce, 506 Duffy Street, Aberdeen, WA 98520; (206)532-1924.

WHERE ELSE TO SEE MIGRATING SHOREBIRDS

WASHINGTON

Willapa National Wildlife Refuge, southwestern Washington: Willapa Bay, one of four major shorebird staging areas on the West Coast, is one of the largest undisturbed estuaries in the western United States. The best views of shorebirds are from Leadbetter Point at the end of the Long Beach Peninsula.

To get to Leadbetter Point from Aberdeen, drive south on U.S. Highway 101 to Seaview. Turn north on State Route 103. Leadbetter Point State Park is at the end of the road.

For more information, contact the Willapa National Wildlife Refuge, Ilwaco, WA 98624; (206)484-3482. For information on area facilities, contact the Long Beach Peninsula Visitors' Bureau, P.O. Box 562, Long Beach, WA 98631; (206)642-2400.

Dungeness Spit National Wildlife Refuge, northwestern Washington: This is not a staging area, but large numbers of migrating shorebirds, including sandpipers, dunlins, turnstones, and phalaropes, do stop to rest and feed on this natural, 5-mile-long sand spit.

To get to Dungeness Spit National Wildlife Refuge from Sequim, go west on U.S. Highway 101 about 4½ miles and then turn north on Kitchen–Dick Lane. In about 3 miles, turn right on Lotzgesell Road. Enter the refuge through the Dungeness Recreation Area.

For more information, contact the Washington Coastal Refuges Office, 33 Barr Road S., Port Angeles, WA 98362; (206)457-8451. For information on area facilities, contact the Sequim Chamber of Commerce, P.O. Box 907, Sequim, WA 98382; (206)683-6197.

OREGON

Bayocean Peninsula, northwestern Oregon: The best spring shorebird viewing at Bayocean Peninsula, a long, thin sand spit, is at high tide. Keep an eye open for killer whales in the bay.

To get to Bayocean Peninsula from Tillamook, drive west on Netarts Highway a little over a mile to Bayocean Road. Follow Bayocean Road north about 5 miles to the spit road.

The peninsula is not a park or refuge, but for general information, try calling Tillamook County offices at (503)322-3477. For information on area facilities, contact the Tillamook Chamber of Commerce, 3705 Highway 101 N., Tillamook, OR 97141; (503)842-7525.

Bullards Beach State Park, southwestern Oregon: Bandon Marsh National Wildlife Refuge is directly across the Coquille River from Bullards Beach State Park. Shorebirds feed on the muddy riverbank, and turnstones and oystercatchers can be seen on the Coquille River jetty. Access into the refuge is difficult, so the best viewing is from the Bullards Beach picnic area and boat launch or from a canoe.

To get to Bullards Beach State Park from Coos Bay, drive south on U.S. Highway 101. One mile north of Bandon, turn west into the park.

For more information, contact Bullards Beach State Park, Box 25, Bandon, OR 97411; (503)347-2209. For information on area facilities, contact the Bandon Chamber of Commerce, P.O. Box 1515, Bandon, OR 97411; (503)347-9616.

CHAPTER 4

TRAIL OF THE KIGER
Mustangs Near Steens Mountain, Oregon

I snagged my arm trying to get the gate fastened back up. It was one of those range gates—four strands of barbed wire with three juniper sticks stuck on for uprights and one real post on the end. Loose loops of wire strung around the top and bottom of the sturdily planted fence post held the gate post closed. I had unhooked the floppy contraption, laid it off to one side of the dusty road, and driven through. Seven big, red beef cows with plastic ear tags watched me try to stretch the gate back across the road. I planted the bottom of the post in the lower loop and, forgetting, let the wire lean against my arm as I struggled the top loop of the gate into place.

The scrape is almost healed now and I sort of like the way it looks—a thin, white streak on tan. It makes me feel a little wild. Feral, really—escaped from domestication and asserting my independence, just like the wild horses I was looking for in the high desert country of southeastern Oregon.

An estimated 50,000 to 75,000 wild horses roam parts of ten western states. Oregon is home to about 2,000; there are no wild horses in Washington. Strictly speaking, they're feral animals, not wildlife—but only because North America's original wild horses died out thousands of years ago under mysterious circumstances.

North America is the horse's original stomping ground: fossils of *Eohippus*, the 50-million-year-old, foot-tall "dawn horse," have been found in Texas and Wyoming. By the time of the latest ice age, *Eohippus* had grown into the modern horse and had spread across the world. But about 8,000 to 10,000 years ago, horses, as well as camels, giant sloths, and other large mammals, disappeared from this hemisphere. Scientists think a number of factors were probably involved and can't say for sure what led to the extinctions.

Spanish explorers reintroduced the horse to America in the 1500s, when they brought their resilient breeds across the ocean suspended from slings in ships. Horses carried the Conquistadors along the Mississippi River and into the Southwest.

Of all the wild horses in the West, Oregon's Kiger mustangs are thought to be among the purest descendants of the original Spanish horses because they show a strong predominance of the dun factor—colors and markings common to many of the original Spanish bloodlines. Dun factor colors are primarily dun (grayish brown), red dun, buckskin, and grulla (true mouse gray, not a mix of black and white hairs), and the distinctive markings include zebralike striping on the legs, bars on the chest, bicolored manes and tails, dorsal stripes, and outlined ears. Somewhat smaller than other wild horses, Kiger mustangs look a lot like the pictures preteen girls draw of horses, with wide-set eyes, long, flowing manes and tails, flared nostrils, and curved ears.

The main Kiger Herd Management Area (HMA) is about sixty miles southeast of Burns, just east of the whistlestop of Diamond. A small viewpoint parking area scuffed out at the top of an unnamed ridge within the HMA lies behind two wire gates (leave them open if they're open, and closed if they're closed) and down eleven miles of dirt road off an out-of-the-way gravel road. The dirt road is deemed unsafe for passenger cars, but I made it in my two-wheel-drive Toyota pickup. I did wonder about my judgment a couple of times, however, especially when the road tipped sideways right where the hill falls away. (Don't drive the road in any vehicle if it looks like rain; wet weather turns the top layer of dust to grease.) The land was alternately humped and smoothed—textured by rocks, sagebrush, grass, scattered troops of juniper, and an occasional grove of aspen trees.

The day before, I had seen a small band of wild palominos at Palomino Buttes, southeast of Riley, and I had seen eighteen or twenty wild horses on the west side of Steens Mountain. The Steens Mountain horses were a lot easier to get to—a black Volvo with New York license plates passed going the other way—but Kiger mustangs carry ghosts of the past. A bad road was minor dues for the ultimate wild horse quest.

No one was at the parking area, and I probably could have waited a week for someone to show up. Squat clouds with dark gray bottoms were stacking up, and an afternoon breeze cooled the tumbles of basalt boulders scattered among purple lupines. Thick, gray-trunked junipers tufted with chartreuse wolf lichen looked like they were finished growing and had given themselves over purely to meditation. Through the silence came single sounds: one bird, a mosquito, the wind. I ate the last of the yogurt from my cooler and remembered for the first time in a long time that people need food to live. Pouring water from a five-gallon jug into a smaller water bottle, I didn't spill a drop.

A short trail marked by rock cairns took off from the parking area. I was simply happy to be there and half didn't expect to see any horses. It's big country, and effort doesn't guarantee reward in most endeavors—especially in wildlife watching. But a short way down the trail, buckskin flashed on the hillside across the way, and there they were—a herd of Kiger mustangs kegged up in the shade, nosed in like spokes around the tree trunks, their bicolored tails swishing.

I counted thirty-one horses and two new babies. Late spring is a good time to look for mustangs. Foals are at their mothers' sides, and stallions are full of the pomp and posture of the approaching breeding season. (Mating takes place within two weeks after a mare has given birth.) Most aggressive interactions between stallions are merely showy displays, with a few nips or kicks thrown in for effect, but occasionally fights escalate into screaming, ripping, bloody battles.

Wild horses are highly gregarious animals that live in small family bands. It is not unusual, however, for bands to join into a temporary herd on good grazing land or when there is danger.

A dun mare drifted out from under the trees, followed by a foal who looked to be concentrating on which foot to pick up in what order. The midday siesta apparently over, horses spread out over the hillside to graze. It was hard to tell, but I guessed there were four to six bands in all.

Most bands consist of a dominant stallion, his harem of one to eleven or more mares, and their offspring. Bands are very stable and remain together all year. Colts usually leave when they are about two years old to join a bachelor band, where they stay for a few years until they can manage to collect their own harem. When they reach breeding age, fillies often wander, or may be pushed, from their band of origin and are quickly picked up by another stallion.

Weaving his outstretched neck like a snake, his ears laid back, head close to the ground, the stallion keeps band members under his authority. Some researchers think that it is the drive to dominate, not sexual desire, that motivates a stallion to be proprietary. Mares come into heat only in the spring, when forage is most plentiful, but studs expend a lot of energy keeping the band intact all year. A stallion will sometimes tolerate the presence of another adult male in his band, as long as the second male is willing to take a subordinate role. In such cases, the second stallion may be a confederate from bachelor days. Horses form long-term friendships with other individuals of similar age and rank. Friends graze and water together, rest their heads on one another's backs, and groom one another.

It takes some effort to look at horses without drawing humans into the picture. After all, our relationship goes back some 5,000 years to when people first began using horses to pull their carts and chariots. Horses had a profound influence on Native American culture. Brutalized by Conquistadors on horseback, Indians eventually began to retaliate by stealing the Spaniards' mounts. Horse meat was a favored food until the animal's higher value was recognized. Many tribes of Native Americans quickly developed superb riding skills. Their lives were transformed as more efficient hunting and traveling allowed leisure time for cultural development, including art and sport, and for war. For a time, native societies flourished.

With a different attitude than Europeans toward the accumulation of possessions, Native Americans allowed large numbers of horses to wander away; they could get more when they needed them. Over the years, continuous raids and relaxed custody seeded the West with wild-roaming horses. The Northwest's wild horses likely originated from horses lost or stolen from Spanish missions in California and Mexico. Around the mid-1800s, 2 million to 7 million mustangs roamed the West. By the turn of the century, more horses had escaped from homesteaders, and well-bred stallions furnished by the federal government were purposely released by ranchers to mingle with wild herds to improve stock for cavalry use.

In the first half of the twentieth century, hundreds of thousands of wild horses were rounded up and put to service in World War I. Hundreds of thousands more were killed by ranchers, game managers, and the Taylor Grazing Service (a federal agency that later evolved into the Bureau of Land Management), which saw the horses as competing with livestock and big game animals. "Mustangers" rounded up wild horses and burros to be processed into dog food, fertilizer, and chicken feed.

After seeing a bloody foal trampled to death in the back of a mustanger's truck, a Reno secretary named Velma Johnston made wild horses her life's cause. "Wild Horse Annie," as she came to be known, was responsible for the passage of two federal laws protecting wild horses and burros. The first, enacted in 1959 and often referred to as the "Wild Horse Annie Act," prohibited the use of airplanes and motor vehicles in wild horse roundups and banned the poisoning of waterholes. Still, by 1969 fewer than 17,000 wild horses remained on western ranges. Wild Horse

Annie organized a children's letter-writing campaign, and in 1971 the Wild Free-Roaming Horse and Burro Act was passed, outlawing the killing, capture, or harassment of horses or burros by private citizens on federal lands. Asked one time what kept her going, the ninety-eight-pound woman replied, "A tight girdle and a case of hair spray." Wild Horse Annie died in 1977.

The protections worked, and the question has now become what to do with increasing populations. Horses compete with cattle and wildlife for edible vegetation, and too many wild horses on a range can destroy habitat as readily as can too many cattle or domestic sheep. Across the West, mustang herds are increasing about 20 percent a year, and wildlife conservationists, ranchers, and the government agree numbers must be controlled.

Wild horses and burros can be adopted from the Bureau of Land Management, the agency charged with wild horse management, but the money collected through the Adopt-A-Horse program falls far short of the amount needed to run the program. Although more than 100,000 excess wild horses and burros have been removed from western ranges and adopted since 1973, there are more animals than adopters, so other means of population control, including antifertility drugs, are being studied.

All of Oregon's eighteen wild horse herd management areas have set minimum and maximum population numbers that are maintained primarily by regular roundups. Horses removed from the range in these roundups are put up for adoption. The Kiger herd in the Kiger HMA is kept between fifty-one and eighty-two horses. A second Kiger herd in another herd management area is kept between thirty-three and fifty-six.

I watched through binoculars as the dun mare nursed her foal, and I tried to pick out which of the other mares were pregnant. Some of the horses were grooming one another, an activity that keeps them clean and free of parasites and, equally important, satisfies their desire to be sociable. The ritual often follows a routine in which the horses stand face to tail and work their way along, biting burrs out of each other's manes, then nipping along the neck and back, finishing off at the root of the tail. Stallions rarely relax enough to enjoy such a session.

While the stallion is clearly the dominant force in each band, a mare may occasionally rebel. Once her mind is set, she will go nostril to nostril with the stallion in her refusal to be herded against her will. She's not fighting for dominance, just to get her way. Foals are usually a factor in any recalcitrance. The mare may not be ready to rejoin the band after having her baby, or if a foal is sick or weak she may refuse to leave it when the stallion is ready to move on.

Each band has a recognized lead mare who is usually older and more experienced than the other females. The lead mare selects the direction and route the band takes when fleeing danger. In most cases, the stallion runs at the status position in the rear, where he can push and protect his band, but he will take the lead if the band is under extreme pressure.

Not all previously domesticated animals who escape from human control can survive in the wild. Poodles, for instance, probably wouldn't make it. But for many of the horses that found their way back into the Wild West, domestication appears to have been only saddle-blanket deep. Indeed, one of the first things wild horses do for a recently liberated new member is chew off its halter.

Ron Harding, a wild horse program manager for the Bureau of Land Management and a lifelong horseman, says wild horses are different from the domestic variety. "I've had horses all my life. Thought I knew 'em," he said. "Then I got my first wild one. It looked like a horse all right, but it took me a couple of years of letting go—little by little—of what I thought I knew. By the time I was done, I had thrown out a lot."

For one thing, says Harding, wild horses are a lot smarter. Nobody feeds and waters them so they have to think for themselves. As a result, where it may take a pure-bred quarter horse colt three to four weeks to respond to training, a wild foal might get the point in as little as forty-five minutes. Mares and foals are accustomed to being bossed around by the stallion. They expect to be dominated, or at least directed, Harding hypothesizes. He looked at me a little sideways when he said that, maybe thinking I would kick him, or dig in my heels and refuse to leave his office. I took the bit in my teeth and smiled.

I thought about it later as I sat and watched the Kiger mustangs. Humans, and maybe animals coping with unnatural living arrangements in zoos, are the only creatures that seem to tinker with social order. For us humans, it hasn't settled down since Adam and Eve got naked.

But there is no mare liberation movement. Social order, at least in the animal world, is usually the way it is because that's what works for all concerned.

I got lonesome sitting there, watching the best friends groom and the baby nurse. If I could have written my own social order on the spot, I would have written myself right into that buckskin band and stood around with my foot tipped while somebody rubbed a head against my back.

There I go again. It's hard to look at horses without trying to draw humans into the picture.

Timing Your Visit: Late spring is a good time to look for wild horses. Foals are with their mothers, and stallions are feisty with the approaching breeding season. Also, most roads are dried out and open by then.

Contact: For more information on Oregon's wild horses or the Adopt-A-Horse program, contact the Bureau of Land Management (BLM), Burns District Office, HC 74-12533 Highway 20 W., Hines, OR 97738; (503)573-5241.

Getting There: Stop by the BLM office first to check on road conditions and buy any maps you may need. To get to the district office from Burns, take Highway 20 west and in less than 5 miles, you will see the office on the left side of the highway.

To get to the Kiger Herd Management Area viewpoint from Burns, take Highway 205 south about 35 miles to the Diamond cutoff. Follow the gravel Diamond–Grain Camp Road about 16 miles through Diamond (a whistlestop with a roadhouse hotel, store, and gas pump) and on to the viewing area turnoff. Past Diamond, the washboard road takes some steep turns with no guard rail. The 11-mile road up to the viewing area is rough and not recommended for passenger cars. Don't go if it looks like rain; precipitation makes the top layer of dust very slippery. If you're already at the viewing area and it begins to rain, wait there until the road dries out a bit. Afternoon storms are short and the dry ground soaks up moisture fast.

See the suggestions below for easier-to-reach locations for viewing wild horses in the same general region as the Kiger area.

Accommodations: For information on area facilities, contact the Harney County Chamber of Commerce, 18 West D Street, Burns, OR 97720; (503)573-2636.

WHERE ELSE TO SEE WILD HORSES

WASHINGTON

Ellensburg Rodeo: There may not be any wild horses in Washington, but the eighth-largest rodeo in the world is held in Ellensburg in late August/early September.

To get to Ellensburg from Seattle, take I-90 east. The rodeo is held at the Kittitas County Fairgrounds.

For more information on the rodeo or on area facilities, contact the Ellensburg Chamber of Commerce, 436 N. Sprague, Ellensburg, WA 98926; (206)925-3137.

OREGON

Steens Mountain, southeastern Oregon: Up to several hundred horses roam the Steens Mountain Herd Management Area, which is spread over 250,000 rugged acres. Roads are passable but slow. Always leave gates as you find them.

To get to the Steens Mountain HMA from Burns, take Highway 205 south through Frenchglen to the South Steens Mountain Loop Road. Follow the gravel loop road east about 6 miles and start scanning the hillsides for the next 8 or so miles. In early spring, the loop road is closed at Blitzen River crossing.

For more information on the Steens Mountain wild horses contact the BLM, Burns District Office, HC 74-12533 Highway 20 W., Hines, OR 97738; (503)573-5241. For information on area facilities, contact the Harney County Chamber of Commerce, 18 West D Street, Burns, OR 97720; (503)573-2636.

Palomino Buttes, southeastern Oregon: Yes, there are palominos at Palomino Buttes.

To get to the Palomino Buttes area from Burns, head west on Highway 20 about 16 miles to Double O Road (County Road 133).

About 11 miles south on Double O Road there is a faint track road running to the west. The road is very rough, but in under 2 miles you will reach a small reservoir stock pond that the horses, as well as shorebirds and cattle, often frequent.

For information on Palomino Buttes horses, contact the BLM, Burns District Office, HC 74-12533 Highway 20 W., Hines, OR 97738; (503)573-5241. For information on area facilities, contact the Harney County Chamber of Commerce, 18 West D Street, Burns, OR 97720; (503)573-2636.

CHAPTER 5

WATER BABIES

Harbor Seals, Pups, and Sea Lions at Cape Arago, Oregon

Watching seal mothers and pups bobbing together in the swells, I'm filled with childhood memories of Florida vacations: my own mother and I, floating in a loose embrace, lifted and dropped gently by the sea—an intimate, saltwater warm front captured between stiff bathing suit and bare chest.

The harbor seal mothers and pups here in Oregon's North Cove at Cape Arago State Park arrange themselves in a similar fashion, hanging face to face in vertical pairs, gazing over each other's shoulders or nibbling on each other's lips. Sets of big-face, little-face dot the water of the bay.

Farther out, loud sea-lion barks, growls, and raucous rasp-berries stream from Shell Island, sitting like a nose over the cove's mouth. Shell Island and its associate Simpson Reef distract the sea's power, making North Cove more a place of surge than of surf. A perfect place for mothers and babies.

Harbor seals come here to bear their young. Steller sea lions, elephant seals, and gangs of bachelor California sea lions also visit the little cove, which is pressed into a cliff on the north side of Cape Arago. The beach lies in a crescent at the bottom of a steep trail and a thick lane of driftwood runs along the bottom of the bluff. Topsoil rides the clifftop like a receding hairline. As waves draw lace curtains of yellowed sea foam across flat black rocks, seals cork and roll within clear view. Humans are conspicuous here, outsiders stumbling through some other family's reunion.

Seals are curious by nature, and one trailed my progress along the short smile of beach. It would raise its head higher out of the water when I waved to it. Others less interested in my presence tilted their heads back into the water like women trying to get their hair wet without mussing their makeup. I watched these individuals more closely, thinking they might be nursing sub-merged pups. Across the cove, the noses of sleeping seals buoyed on the water like upside-down black cups.

front flipper of harbor seal

About halfway down the beach I almost tripped over a dead seal that had been offered up by the tides. It looked like one more rock or drift log. I stopped to count its thick whiskers and admire the fine claws on its front flippers. It didn't look like it had been there long, but I resisted touching the gray fur. Dead animals are a natural part of the beach ecology, but because they may carry parasites, it's wise not to touch them when you stop to look and pay your respects.

Of the five furred and flippered marine mammals—pin-nipeds—that can be seen in Oregon, North Cove is missing only the fur seal, which is rarely seen near shore while in Northwest waters. The other four species—harbor seals, elephant seals, Steller sea lions, and California sea lions—can all be seen at one time or another from the North Cove viewpoint off the Cape Arago Highway across from Simpson Reef. While all species spend at least part of the year here, only the harbor seal and Steller sea lion breed in the Pacific Northwest.

The word *pinniped* comes from the Greek *pinna* (wing) and Latin *pedis* (foot), and is used to identify members of the order Pinnipedia, which includes seals, sea lions, and walruses. Sea otters, which have paws instead of flippers, are in an altogether different order which they share with weasels, skunks, and river otters.

Except for the walrus, which is in a class by itself, the pinnipeds are divided into two families: the true seals and the eared seals. True seals, such as harbor seals and elephant seals, have no external ear flaps. Eared seals, as you may have guessed, have external ear flaps. Steller sea lions, California sea lions, and fur seals (which are really more like sea lions than seals) all have what look like little squirrel ears.

Harbor seals are the most abundant and familiar of all the Northwest pinnipeds. The National Marine Fisheries Service estimates the total population off the Oregon and Washington coasts at about 16,500. They are also the most visible, not just because of their numbers, but because of their affinity for resting out of the water on sandy beaches, mudflats, and other onshore spots. Harbor seals are also often seen near river mouths and on low rocks along the shoreline. The other pinnipeds rarely rest onshore, although California sea lions aren't shy about pulling themselves up onto navigation buoys, ferry docks, and other floating structures within sight of humans.

It is the harbor seal's preference for near-shore or onshore habitat that makes it possible to see mothers with their pups. Although Steller sea lions also breed in Oregon, they tend to stay on offshore rocks, out of easy view. In contrast, harbor seals with babies seek out protected beaches, bays, harbors, and gently sloping rocky shores.

Although harbor seals do not typically migrate long distances to breeding grounds or gather in large, cohesive groups as do many other pinnipeds, they do seem to congregate at traditional nursery and haul-out sites during the spring pupping season. "Hauling out" couldn't be a more apt description of the way the neckless, short-flippered creatures hump themselves out of the water to rest on land like overturned Saabs.

Not much is known about harbor seal courtship, but it must be low-key, at least when compared to the breeding season battles waged by elephant seal or sea lion bulls fighting over territory and females. The male harbor seal's involvement is apparently limited to the act of insemination. (While all eared seal males collect harems, the elephant seal is the only true seal that does.)

Most harbor seal pups are born in April and May, although pupping may be a month or two later in the inland waters of Washington's Puget Sound. Harbor seals breed within a month after giving birth, even though implantation of the fertilized egg may be delayed for up to two months. Females have one pup, which nurses for three to six weeks on fat-rich milk, often more than doubling its fifteen-pound birth weight in that period. Mothers occasionally stash premature or weak pups on the beach while they hunt for food. Every year, some of these beach babies die, not because they've been abandoned—which chances are they haven't—but because people think they have. Well-intentioned humans snatch young seals off the beach believing they have "rescued" them, when in fact the act more often leads to death for the baby and anxiety for the parent.

Your most responsible, and most difficult, response is to cut a wide swath around any seal pup you may see and leave it alone. The mother will probably be back soon and may already be waiting nearby for you to leave so she can collect her offspring. If the baby is still alone and in obvious distress should you check back at the end of the day, call the Oregon State Police or, in Washington, the Washington State Patrol. They will contact wildlife workers, who will care for the animal until it can be released back into the wild.

The curious seal was still trailing me as I neared the far end of the North Cove beach. Its face was at once sweet and skull-like. Seals' corneas are less convex than those of land mammals, lending their huge, lashless, black eyes a Little Orphan Annie look.

It's against wildlife-watching etiquette to approach animals too closely, but I can't find any rules against letting them come to you. More than any other species of wildlife that comes to mind, except maybe gray whales in Baja, seals seem to be fascinated by humans. Seals and some sea lions will approach and follow a slow-moving boat. From a drifting sea kayak, you can hear them breathing behind you as they make their study. They seem to show even greater interest if you whistle or talk to them.

Don't feel silly to try it. The queen of England herself is said to talk to seals. Years ago, *News of the World* reported that "After she had bought the Castle of Mey in Caithness, Queen Elizabeth became an expert at finding the tiny coral-pink cowrie shells known as 'Groatie buckies' in the sand of the lonely shore. She never tires of watching the seals, and was enchanted when, by singing Scottish ballads to them, she brought them closer and closer inshore to listen."

Sea lions, especially the more aloof Steller, may be slightly less responsive to folk songs. Spotted on Shell Island from the viewpoint up on the Cape Arago Highway, the one-ton Steller bull staked out on the beach looked as disinterested and unapproachable as a surveillant sphinx. The bull appeared gargantuan in comparison to the harbor seals dotting the periphery of the island and was visibly larger than the California sea lions lounging nearby. But even the Steller bull would have been dwarfed had a seventeen-foot-long, 6,000-pound elephant seal come along and decided to haul its mass out of the water.

Looking at the jumble of pinnipeds on Shell Island through binoculars, I didn't see any elephant seals, but even from a distance, the lighter-colored Stellers—both male and female—were relatively easy to distinguish from the dark California sea lions. The squat gray harbor seals were a snap. Through the general babble, the Steller's throaty roar, seldom used outside the breeding season, was clearly discernible from the California sea lion's persistent, nonstop bark. The seals were silent. All three species seemed to be quite tolerant of each other on the tiny island's crowded space of beach.

Steller sea lions don't establish breeding colonies at Cape Arago, but at more isolated places along the coast, bulls fight each other each spring to establish territories and collect harems of ten to twenty cows. After the initial period of sometimes ferocious fighting, they maintain their status through less violent but no less intimidating displays and vocalizations. Defending bulls generally refuse to leave their territories while the females are bearing and nursing young and so may not eat for two months.

Steller pups are born in May and early June. Like harbor seals, female Stellers mate within weeks of giving birth, and implantation of the fertilized egg may be delayed for up to two months.

Courtship style might be at the root of several generalized differences between most true seals (which worldwide include the harp seal, bearded seal, ribbon seal, monk seal, and leopard seal) and sea lions. Female Stellers, as well as the females of other harem-collecting species, are much smaller than the males, but the female and male of species such as the harbor seal, which have one brief tryst and call it good, are close in size.

Sea lions are also far more vocal, a trait that allows the males to substitute voice displays for violence once their territory has been won. Without a territory to defend, and no need to interact aggressively, seals can afford to be quiet.

Seals and sea lions are also set apart by how they move. Sea lions, with their long front flippers and the ability to rotate their rear flippers forward, can walk on all fours in a galumphing gait. They are relatively agile out of the water and can charge, chase, fight, and lord it around quite well. In contrast, seals' back flippers don't rotate, and they have to be flat on their bellies for both short front flippers to be in contact with the ground. On land they move by undulating their bodies—an amazing sight when they're in a hurry.

While you may visit North Cove to see mother and baby seals, the California sea lions are pretty cheerful to watch as they horse around in the water. Because of the sea lions' intelligence, even temperament, and propensity for play, they are the species most commonly used to provide entertainment for humans.

Most of the California sea lions lingering on the Northwest coast are bachelor males too young to win a territory at home in California or Mexico. Their behavior reflects that of a stereotypical unattached young male: they eat, sleep, and goof around. They love to body-surf and will pass a North Cove afternoon catching wave after wave. You can take the sea lion out of California . . . When they're not surfing, a group may float on the surface, rafted together with their flippers raised like little black spinnakers. The hoisted flipper works like a radiator to help regulate body heat. All California sea lions go south for the breeding season. They begin leaving the Northwest in May and are gone by early summer, but small numbers begin to reappear in August.

Since coming under the shield of the Marine Mammal Protection Act (MMPA) of 1972, the California sea lion population has been growing about 6 percent a year to a current estimated population of 80,000 to 90,000 spread between Alaska and California. There may be that many more in Baja, Mexico. Tension is growing between some humans, fishermen in particular, and the increasingly abundant California sea lions. Both sport and commercial fishermen complain that sea lions are stealing enough fish off their lines and out of their nets to have an impact on their livelihoods or recreation. While this may be true, it probably wouldn't seem like such a problem if humans and sea lions weren't fighting over a smaller and smaller salmon pie. Habitat loss, dams, gill nets, and overfishing have a greater cumulative effect on salmon runs than marine mammals ever will.

Some other pinniped species, all of which are protected under the MMPA, are also rebounding from dismally low numbers left by market hunters at the turn of the century, although none have matched the expansion of California sea lions.

Along with the MMPA, Steller sea lions are also protected by the Endangered Species Act. Although Steller populations in Oregon have remained fairly stable since the 1960s, California's population is down, and Alaska's population decreased 60 percent between 1985 and 1989. The National Marine Fisheries Service points to a diminishing supply of food in the ocean, incidental kills by domestic and foreign fisheries, and deliberate shootings as possible factors contributing to the decline. Oregon has a breeding population of about 2,500 Stellers, and worldwide population estimates range from less than 100,000 to 300,000.

Expanding sea lion numbers are a testament to the fact that protections can work to rebuild wildlife populations. And, increasing complaints of competition for fish resources testify to the fact that some humans resent sharing the top of the food chain.

We will face similar dilemmas as we succeed in restoring other species that may compete with us—such as wolves on rangelands—or species that threaten our sense of security—like bears in the suburbs or cougars in greenbelts. I like to think there's room at the top for all of us, even if we have to rebalance our economic, social, and political values. It will take work and some creative problem solving, but it's worth it because living with wildlife sure beats living without it.

Timing Your Visit: Along the Oregon Coast, late April through May are good months for seeing harbor seals and pups, Steller sea lions, elephant seals, and California sea lions.

Contact: For more information on seals and sea lions, contact the Mark O. Hatfield Marine Science Center, Newport, OR 97365; (503)867-0100.

Getting There: To get to Cape Arago State Park's North Cove from Coos Bay, take the Empire-Coos Bay Highway to the Cape Arago Highway and continue south. North Cove is about 14 miles southwest of Coos Bay. Watch for the viewpoint pull-out at the north end of the cove. The steep trail down to the North Cove beach begins from a large parking area a short distance farther south on the Cape Arago Highway.

Accommodations: For campsite reservations or information, contact Sunset Bay State Park, 13030 Cape Arago Highway, Coos Bay, OR 97420; (503)888-4902. For information on other area facilities, contact the Coos Bay/North Bend Bay Area Chamber of Commerce, 50 E. Central, Coos Bay, OR 97420; (800)762-6278, or outside Oregon, (800)824-8486.

WHERE ELSE TO SEE HARBOR SEALS AND PUPS AND SEA LIONS

WASHINGTON
Washington State Ferry System, San Juan Islands, Washington: Take a ferry ride through the San Juan Islands of Puget Sound and watch the shoreline for seals and sea lions hauled out on beaches and rocks or even the ferry dock. For a day trip or an overnighter, try leaving your vehicle behind to avoid long ferry lines and save money. Walk or bike instead.

Catch the Friday Harbor ferry from Anacortes at the north end of Whidbey Island. To get there from Seattle, take I-5 north to the Anacortes exit and follow signs to the ferry.

For Washington State Ferry information, call (206)464-6400. For information on facilities in the San Juan Islands, contact the San Juan Islands Visitor Information Center, P.O. Box 65, Lopez, WA 98261; (206)468-3663.

Dungeness Spit National Wildlife Refuge, Olympic Peninsula, Washington: Dungeness Spit extends more than 5 miles into the Strait of Juan de Fuca. The lee side of the spit forms a quiet lagoon favored by seals.

To get to Dungeness Spit National Wildlife Refuge from Sequim, go west on U.S. Highway 101 about 4½ miles and then turn north on Kitchen–Dick Lane. In about 3 miles, turn right onto Lotzgesell Road. Enter the refuge through the Dungeness Recreation Area.

For more information on the refuge, contact the Dungeness Spit National Wildlife Refuge in care of the Nisqually National Wildlife Refuge, 100 Brown Farm Road, Olympia, WA 98506; (206)753-9467. For information on area facilities, contact the Sequim/Dungeness Valley Chamber of Commerce, P.O. Box 907, Sequim, WA 98382; (206)683-6197.

OREGON
Three Arch Rocks National Wildlife Refuge, northern coast of Oregon: Harbor seals and Steller sea lions share these offshore rocks with one of the continent's largest seabird colonies. Good views of Three Arch Rocks refuge can be had from Oceanside Beach State Wayside.

To get to Oceanside Beach State Wayside from Tillamook, take the Bayocean Road north around the Cape Meares thumb.

For more information on Three Arch Rocks refuge, contact the U.S. Fish and Wildlife Service, 1002 N.E. Holladay Street, Portland, OR 97232-4181; (503)231-6828. For information on area facilities, contact the Tillamook Chamber of Commerce, 3705 Highway 101 N., Tillamook, OR 97141; (503)842-7525.

Sea Lion Caves, south-central coast of Oregon: An elevator cut through 208 feet of rock delivers you to a sea-level grotto where you'll find the closest, most unusual view of Steller sea lions you're likely to get without a boat.

To get to the Sea Lion Caves from Florence, take U.S. Highway 101 north and watch for signs.

For more information, contact Sea Lion Caves, 91560 Highway 101, Florence, OR 97439; (503)547-3111. For information on area facilities, contact the Florence Chamber of Commerce, P.O. Box 26000, Highway 101, Florence, OR 97439; (503)997-3128.

SUMMER

CHAPTER 6

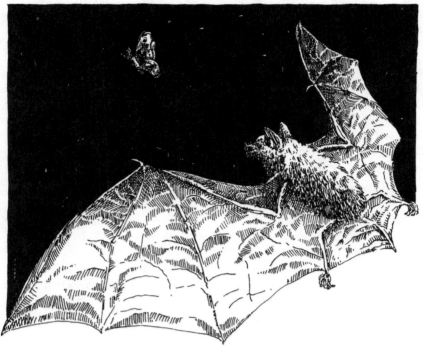

NIGHT MOVES
Bats in the Lava Lands, Oregon

I stand on my deck in the summer twilight and wait for the bats. Twenty minutes before dark, two shadowy forms will swoop in to take over where the swallows left off—climbing, diving, circling—chasing mosquitoes with aerobatic aplomb.

The game is to stand perfectly still and let them buzz me. Six feet is the current record; I'm shooting for three. They approach from far across the yard in a doodling flight path, starting high and working low. The first one makes a pass over the birdbath, gains altitude, and then dips toward the house. Toward me, standing on the deck, waiting. It pulls up with seconds to spare, flashing a caricatured form familiar from Dracula movies and trick-or-treat bags. I've been crazy about bats ever since I saw a mother bat with her baby on television. She was hanging from a cave roof with the baby at her breast and in a quick motion drew her wings around the two of them like shrink-wrap.

It's hard to fit my backyard bats into the urban wildlife category. They're too mysterious, too independent. They would never eat the dogfood on the porch. So whenever I see bats in a civilized setting, such as my yard or a city park, I connect them to the bats in central Oregon's Lava Lands, an area south of Bend that is tunneled with lava tubes, jumbled with piles of volcanic rock, and blessed with bats. In my mind I carry a sand painting, gray and black, with subtle hues of purple and dark green. The bats, small smudges over the flat landscape, infuse the image with a joyful wildness.

The Lava Lands area offers more to the bat fan than silhouettes at night. At the High Desert Museum, a group of pallid bats lives in a display made to look like the corner of a barn. From outside the glass you can watch them yawn in the red light and shuffle their dozing huddle. Six of the soft-looking bats could fit into half a cantaloupe. And down the road from the museum, Lava River Cave offers the opportunity to slip into some darkness and experience cave ecology firsthand. Lava River Cave is the longest uncollapsed lava tube known in Oregon. Bats use it, and although they're almost impossible to spot while you're in the tube (they hide in the far reaches), you can see them around the entrance at dawn and dusk. The emergence isn't spectacular but it will get your mental sand painting started. Because we don't have big caves in the Northwest, you have to travel to a place like Bracken Cave in Texas to see the truly impressive cave fly-outs. There, every night, millions of Mexican free-tailed bats prematurely darken the twilight sky as they flow from the cave.

Fortunately, you don't need caves to find bats. Quite a few species roost during the day under peeling bark on old trees, in the cavities of snags, under bridges, in abandoned structures, or under the eaves of occupied buildings. At night when they're not hunting insects, bats haunt separate eating roosts, which are usually more out in the open than the day roosts. It used to puzzle me to find a single moth wing, sans body, on the ground until I discovered that the wings are the likely litter from a bat meal. When a bat catches a moth, it takes its first bite from the abdomen, leaving the wings to flutter to the ground. If the moth is more than a mouthful, the bat retreats to its eating roost to consume the bug at leisure. After repeated use of the same eating roost, the ground below begins to look like a wing midden. So add "piles of moth wings" to your list of things to look for on nature walks. Good places to check include under big trees, at the entrance to caves or mines, and in rock crevices.

cecropia moth wing

In the Northwest, bat-watching season begins in the spring, when the big brown bat—so named because the four-inch-long creature is one inch larger than the little brown bat—emerges from hibernation. Viewing picks up in the summer, when the bat species that migrate instead of hibernate have returned from Arizona or Mexico. Late summer is a time of increased activity as bats spend more time hunting to gain weight before the winter.

Bats can live just about anywhere they can find water, a roosting place, and bugs to eat. They hunt over ponds, fields, among scattered trees near open spaces, above roadways, and around streetlights. Nighthawks and poorwills also fly at night, but you'll know the bats by their silence and silhouette. Take up a place near the water if you can—bats like to get a drink when they first leave the roost. Flight can slow to almost a hover as they lap at the water's surface. Occasionally, a big bass or trout will crash up and snatch the drinking bat, but this must not be too common because the clerk at the fly-fishing shop thought I was joking when I asked if there were bat-pattern flies.

It's not likely you'll be able to spot bats in caves, and you wouldn't want to disturb their rest anyway. But consider going underground just for the experience. Think of it as the pathway to bat brotherhood—or sisterhood, as the case may be. I rented a propane lantern at the entrance to the Lava River Cave and descended into the valley of darkness. The lava tube starts spaciously but peters out to a crawl space one mile in and a couple of hundred feet down. Caves are not everyone's idea of a good time, but they can double your perspective of the terrain. We are at once in and out of our own element in subterranean spaces. Some people enjoy caves; they feel safe and secure in the earth's dark bedroom. Others can't push themselves deeper than the cave's twilight zone. The darkness is too dark, the spaces too small. Womb or tomb? Perhaps this emotional confusion contributes to the fear and mistrust surrounding bats—dwellers in darkness, livers of secret lives. But of course there's nothing diabolical about a nocturnal lifestyle; it's just an ecological niche on the flip side of day. And with the split shift, bats aren't competing with birds for food and are able to concentrate on their work of insect control and pollination.

Seventy percent of the world's 900 bat species, including all of the 18 or so species of bats in the Northwest, eat insects. Most others feed on fruit or the nectar of flowers, and a small minority of bats eat fish, mice, and birds. An even tinier group laps blood, but you have to travel to Latin America to find any of the three species of vampire bat. If you do go there, don't worry too much—vampires are more of a problem for goats than for people.

Bats are *the* major predator of night-flying insects. Colonies can consume billions of insects every summer, including moth and beetle pests that destroy crops and trees. Residents of Chautauqua, New York, encourage the presence of bats, finding them to be an effective alternative to chemical mosquito control. One little brown bat can eat 600 mosquitoes in an hour. Cruising through the air, the bat emits a steady pulse of high-frequency sound waves, which bounce off objects and return as echoes. These echolocation signals provide details on an object's size, speed, shape, and texture. If the information translates into prey, the bat adjusts its course and speeds the pulse into a "feeding buzz." Intensifying the emission lets it lock on target and tag something as small as a mosquito. I'm not afraid of my backyard bats because if they can count the hairs in a mosquito's nose, they're surely not going to run into a stationary five-foot-three form. I just have to remember not to dodge at the last minute.

Echolocation frequencies are out of our human range of hearing, but bats do occasionally make audible vocalizations, especially when roosting in a group. Bunched inside a hollow tree, they can sound like a basketful of peeping Easter chicks.

After prey has been echolocated, the bat uses its wing like a net to snare insects on the fly. Bugs are captured in the wing tip and transferred to a pouched membrane near the tail. The bat grabs the prey into its mouth from the pouch. The erratic flight pattern so unnerving to people is simply a bat finding, snatching, and eating flying bugs. Just pretend they're fast-forward swallows.

Bats are the only mammal capable of true, sustained flight. Flying squirrels are merely gliders. Birds may be faster, but their feathered wings aren't suited for executing tight maneuvers in rapid series—the kind of gymnastic flight that makes bats such agile airborne hunters. Bat wings are actually modified hands with long, bony fingers webbed together with a tough, skinlike membrane. The name of the scientific order to which bats belong, Chiroptera, comes from the Greek *cheir* for "hand" and *ptera* for "wing."

In looking at pictures of bat wings, visualize the hand within the wing. Pick out each slender finger and the little thumb, which protrudes like a small hook off the crook at the front of the wing. With the wings folded down, the bat uses its hook-thumb together with its feet to crawl over rough surfaces such as cave walls and tree bark.

Size and appearance vary widely among the different species of bats. Flying foxes are the largest, with faces like chihuahuas and wingspans up to six feet. They have large eyes compared to other bats because, as fruit eaters, they rely more on eyesight than echolocation to find food. Unfortunately, we don't have any of these handsome animals in the Northwest; they live almost exclusively in the tropics. At the other end of the scale is Thailand's bumblebee bat, the smallest mammal in the world. In between, there's the leaf-chinned bat, long-tongued bat, ghost-faced, long-legged, and small-footed bats, hairy-winged, silvery-haired bats— and more. Bats, who have some of the finest fur of any mammal, spend a great deal of time grooming and always look marvelous. In Dr. Merlin Tuttle's popular bat books, all the subjects in his incredible photographs look brushed and blow-dried.

The big brown bat is one of the more commonly encountered species in the Northwest and is the only species that hibernates here. Given a choice, big browns select buildings for colonial roost sites and so share habitat more closely with humans than bats who roost in caves or trees. If you want to exclude bats from your house, screen all possible entry points, including eaves and gaps around window air conditioners and chimneys. Use fine-mesh screens because some bats can squeeze through openings as small as a dime. If a bat does come into the house, don't panic. Dr. Tuttle reports that in a lifetime of studying bats he has never been attacked by one—no matter how long he chased it. The commotion and flying brooms of a bat-in-the-house incident make for great family stories, unless you're the bat. But rescues make great stories too.

Most importantly, keep an eye on the bat so that it can't wander into some other part of the house and go to sleep where you can't find it. If you can, close all the doors to the room and open all the windows. It's okay to keep the lights on. Gently encourage the bat to fly so that it can find a window. Try not to scream. If the bat looks sick, it simply could be sleepy with the early stages of hibernation. Bats in this condition can't fly until they've spent a few minutes shivering to get their blood circulating. The shivering is normal, so don't worry. If you can't get the bat to fly out a window, try catching it in a towel. Release it where it will be safe if it needs to think about things for a minute before it takes off. Both cats and owls will eat bats, and dogs may nose-press a sluggish bat to death.

A confused bat may try to bite in self-defense, so never handle one without leather gloves. The notion of bats as rabies carriers has been greatly exaggerated. People are in more danger from bee stings and potluck potato salad gone bad.

Bats don't get a bum rap in all societies. In Eastern cultures bats are symbols of family unity and happiness. The Chinese words for "happiness" and "bat" are homonymous, and word plays in messages of congratulations and good will are common. Bats were stylized in symbols of Chinese heraldry and used in decorative patterns on furniture and clothing. This affirmative attitude didn't transfer to our part of the world, even though bats played a role in United States history. In the nineteenth century, guano (bat droppings) provided the saltpeter used to manufacture gunpowder. Guano-based gunpowder was used in the War of 1812 and in the Civil War. The mining of guano for fertilizer was big business in the southwestern United States in the early twentieth century, but dwindling bat populations and the development of inorganic fertilizers closed most mines. Guano is still, however,

an important fertilizer in developing countries and is used exten-
sively on the world's white and black pepper crops.

Among mammalian species, only humans congregate in larger
numbers than bats. This sociability leaves bats extremely vulnerable. Tens of millions have died in deliberate, large-scale acts of
destruction involving burnings, mass poisonings, and dynamiting.
People kill bats out of fear, ignorance, or wanton vandalism. In
1963, close to 30 million free-tailed bats lived in Arizona's Eagle
Creek Cave. Six years later, the population had declined 99.9 percent to 30,000. The ground outside the cave was littered with
shotgun shells and rifle casings.

Bats, especially those hibernating in caves, are also sensitive to
less extreme disturbance. Across the United States, thousands are
thought to die every winter from intentional and unintentional
disturbance. Enthusiastic but uninformed cavers, hikers, and "par-
tyers" drive bats from hibernacula in winter and cause mothers to
abandon nurseries in the spring. In addition, clearcut logging has
reduced the number of available snags, which provide homes to
bats and birds and the bugs they eat. Availability of suitable roosts
and hibernacula is a controlling factor in population levels. If bats
lose their roosting sites, they will be forced to abandon hundreds
of surrounding square miles. Then who will eat the bugs?

When renovations in Chautauqua, New York, took all the
hiding places away from the town's bats, residents took steps to
woo them back. One way to entice bats into a neighborhood is to
put up bat boxes, which look like those old crank telephones
without any of the hardware. They are open only on the bottom
and are a true puzzle to birds, who think all boxes hung on
houses or trees belong to them.

At the far end of Lava River Cave, I crouched into the final
little space with my hissing propane lamp. I wanted to turn out
the lantern and experience the total absence of light, but I wasn't
sure I could get the mantle relit and I would be lost without
echolocation. I thought about the sunlight a mile back up the
tube and the colorless, eyeless millipedes I had noticed in the
lamplight along the way. I grew up spelunking in the spacious
limestone caverns of Kentucky, but these Northwest holes-
in-the-ground seemed much darker, rougher—more dangerous.
At sixteen, caves were fun. But twenty-two years closer to death,

the air underground felt too still.

Womb or tomb? I tried to remember if I had written down anywhere that I wanted to be cremated and scattered to the four winds at high noon.

Timing Your Visit: The best time to see bats over the Lava Lands is in mid- to late summer.

Contact: For more information on Lava Lands or the Lava River Cave, contact the Lava Lands Visitor Center, 58201 S. Highway 97, Bend, OR 97707; (503)593-2421.

For information on bat conservation or bat boxes, contact Bat Conservation International, P.O. Box 162603, Austin, TX 78716.

Getting There: To get to Lava River Cave from Bend, take Highway 97 about 12 miles south and watch for signs. Lava Lands Visitor Center is a couple of miles farther south on Highway 97.

Accommodations: For information on area facilities, contact the Bend Chamber of Commerce, 63085 N. Highway 97, Bend, OR 97701; (503)382-3221.

WHERE ELSE TO SEE BATS

WASHINGTON
Willapa Bay National Wildlife Refuge, southwestern Washington: One of the best and most accessible views of bats is right at refuge headquarters. According to Willapa rangers, the bats can be downright distracting some evenings. Notice the little pond and habitat edges that have been created to make the grounds attractive to wildlife.

To get to refuge headquarters from Longview, take Highway 4 west. At the junction with U.S. Highway 101, turn south. Refuge headquarters is located right off Highway 101, 8 miles northeast of Seaview.

For more information on the refuge, contact Willapa Bay National Refuge, Ilwaco, WA 98624; (206)484-3482. For information on Long Beach area facilities, contact the Long Beach

Peninsula Visitors' Bureau, P.O. Box 562, Long Beach, WA 98631; (206)642-2400.

Point Defiance Park and Zoo, Tacoma, Washington: For seeing bats up close and during the day, it's hard to beat a zoo. You can't lose at Point Defiance. Check out the fruit bats inside; then, at dusk, wait outside for local bats to begin their nightly rounds over park grounds.

To get to Point Defiance Park and Zoo from I-5 in Tacoma, take the Highway 16 exit (exit 132). From Highway 16, go left at the 6th Avenue exit and then take the next right onto Pearl Street. Follow Pearl Street to the park entrance.

For more information, contact Point Defiance Zoo, 5400 N. Pearl, Tacoma, WA 98407; (206)591-5335. For information on Tacoma area facilities, contact the Tacoma Visitor Information Center, 130 Puyallup Avenue, Tacoma, WA 98421; (206)272-7801.

OREGON

Portland Audubon Sanctuary: Bats as well as birds frequent the Audubon Sanctuary in the northwestern corner of Portland. Station yourself near the pond at dusk for the best chance of seeing bats feeding and drinking. The 160-acre sanctuary is connected by trails to the adjacent Forest Park. The Portland Audubon Society chapter, whose headquarters and bookstore are located at the sanctuary, offers a variety of programs (bats are one of the most popular topics) and informational materials on bats, bat boxes, and other wildlife.

To get to the sanctuary from Portland, take Lovejoy Street to Cornell Road and turn right (you will see signs to Pittock Bird Sanctuary). Sanctuary headquarters is on the right, one-tenth of a mile past the second tunnel.

For more information on the sanctuary, contact the Portland Audubon Society, 5151 N.W. Cornell Road, Portland, OR 97210; (503)292-6855. For information on Portland area facilities, contact the Portland/Oregon Visitors Center, 26 S.W. Salmon, Portland, OR 97204; (503)222-2223, or outside Oregon, (800)345-3214.

Oregon Caves National Monument, southwestern Oregon: At Oregon Caves, a naturalist-guide steers the way through a maze of rooms, grottoes, passageways, and "chapels," which over the course of a year may be used by eight species of bats. The cave tour is not recommended for anyone with heart, breathing, or walking difficulty. The 75-minute tour winds through a little more than half a mile of passageways and climbs about 218 feet, including 550 stairs. No unaccompanied cave explorations are permitted. Children under six must pass a step test in order to accompany the tour; child care is available for kids remaining behind.

To get to Oregon Caves from Grants Pass, take Highway 199 south to Cave Junction. Turn east on Highway 46 to the caves.

For more information about Oregon Caves National Monument, contact monument headquarters, 19000 Caves Highway, Cave Junction, OR 97523; (503)592-3400. For information on Grants Pass area facilities, contact the Grants Pass Visitor and Convention Bureau, P.O. Box 1787, Grants Pass, OR 97526; (800)547-5927.

CHAPTER 7

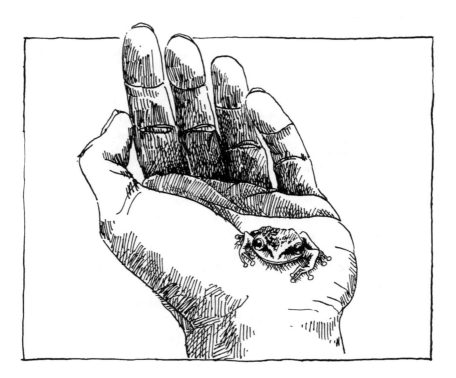

AMPHIBIOUS LANDINGS

Frogs, Salamanders, and Tadpoles in the Gifford Pinchot National Forest, Washington

Everyone should catch a frog at least once in the course of a lifetime. The chase is crashing good fun, and if you succeed, recalling the light feel of frog toes wrapped around your finger can rock you to sleep on any bad night.

Amphibians—frogs, toads, and salamanders—have been around much longer than the pockets to put them in. The class Amphibia evolved 350 million years ago when some fish, bored with the current order, dragged itself out of the water on stumpy fins to test a primitive set of lungs. But even after all these eons, amphibians have skirted total commitment to terra firma. Most species have lungs and legs as adults but are born purely aquatic, outfitted with gills for their life's first phase.

About 3,000 amphibian species have been identified worldwide. We have 32 in the Northwest: 18 salamanders, 10 frogs, and 4 toads. South Prairie marsh in the Gifford Pinchot National Forest is a perfect place for the vacillating vertebrates. In the fifteen-acre pond and nearby creeks and puddles, amphibians can easily trade back and forth between the water and an amphibian-friendly forest floor littered with decaying leaves and rotting logs. Pacific chorus frogs (known until recently as Pacific treefrogs), red-legged frogs, Northwestern salamanders, and Pacific giant salamanders are among the species you can turn up there. If you don't feel like sifting, just sit. Settled on a downed peninsula-of-a-log at the edge of the marsh, I've watched a steady show of frogs breach like fat little killer whales, snatching bugs hovering over the surface.

But don't wait until you get to a wetland in a national forest to start looking. I've caught treefrogs near downtown Seattle and tadpoles in a mud puddle right off Highway 20 near Rainy Pass in the Cascade Mountains. Amphibians are scattered from high-mountain streams to lowland lakes, ponds, and puddles. They lurk in roadside ditches, rotting logs, and rodent dens, hide under rocks on talus slopes, and burrow deep into the ground of sage-brush deserts.

The metamorphosis from aquatic larva to terrestrial adult is what sets true amphibians apart from animals that simply spend a lot of time in the water, such as turtles and crocodiles (both reptiles) and beavers and hippopotamuses (mammals). The term *larva* is used for any juvenile animal that undergoes extreme physiological changes on the way to adulthood. Most frog and toad larvae, better known as tadpoles, look very different from the adults, whereas the salamander larva and adult look quite similar, despite the major difference that one has gills and one has lungs.

Catching and releasing amphibians in our part of the world is generally more dangerous to them than it is to us. None have venomous bites, and none cause—or cure—warts. Many species do, however, emit toxins through their skin as a protection against predators. Toads and newts, which are a type of salamander, are among the most toxic species. Eat a rough-skinned newt and you might die. Cope's giant and Pacific giant salamanders reportedly bite when provoked, but most amphibians resort to scorpionlike poses and poison glands for defense. So caution the kids, watch the dog, and don't kiss any toads. Be forewarned, but don't be put off. Once you've held a frog or salamander close to your face, counted the heartbeats in its throat, and noticed its details of texture, color, and shape, your world will be a more intricate place.

Frogs and toads, "anurans" as they're called when lumped together, are relatively easy to find during breeding season, when they're loud, gathered in groups, and more or less oblivious to such details as intruding humans. Although some frogs look like toads and vice versa, a few generalizations can be made. Frogs are typically slimmer, sleeker, and better jumpers than toads. Toads are more broad-bodied and have skin like a bumpy dill pickle. They're clumsy, can't jump very far, and may be found farther from water than most frogs. A bulging poison gland behind the eye is another toad clue, although the gland shouldn't be confused with a frog's tympanum—the flat, round eardrum disc noticeable on many frogs.

Mating season for both frogs and toads can occur anytime from November to August, depending upon the species and elevation, but even outside the breeding cycle, frogging can be productive on any warm summer night after a rain when humidity is high and bugs, the anuran's favorite food, are abundant. Nighttime frog stalking is best for observing the largest numbers. All you need is a flashlight, rubber boots, an aquarium net, and a smallish body of water with natural edges, decent cover, and a healthy bug population. If you don't hear frogs, try a different place. Try South Prairie.

Reep, reep, reeeeep. Ribbet. Cheep. Cheep. I stood in the grassy muck on the shore of the marsh and listened, headlamp turned on. A mosquito bit my neck. More responsible adults would be sitting at home watching "Cosby" or discussing the pros and cons of refinancing. My boot made a sucking noise as I lifted my foot. The frog chorus had resumed, and I continued making my way toward the sound. When the sound stopped, I stopped. When it started again, so did I. Frog vision is keyed more to movement than shape, so you can get quite close with a little patience. The light doesn't seem to bother them, and I slowly turned my head, sweeping the darkness for eyeshine. Finally, two little beams shone back like signals from space. I bent ever so slowly, reaching . . . reaching . . . reaching . . . frog Tai Chi. The little frog flipped away in midreach. I never caught a frog that night, but I did come home with mosquito bites in the shape of the Big Dipper.

Different frog species have distinctly different voices. Leopard frogs, for example, make a low, guttural chortling and grunting noise that sounds like a motorboat. Western toads have a tittering, cheeping, birdlike sound, and the spadefoot toad *kwa-a-a-ks* like a duck. The call of the green frog has been likened to the plucking of the bass string of a banjo, and Pacific chorus frogs are the ones that go *ribbet*—or *wreck-it,* depending on the translation. To make these vocalizations, a frog clamps its mouth and nostrils shut and forces air from its lungs to its mouth. On each pass, air escapes through slits in the bottom of the mouth into a pouch of skin, which inflates and resonates.

Frogs and toads are particularly loquacious during mating season, when males use their voices to draw females to breeding sites and convey other reproduction-related information. The female's voice is less complex and often limited to defense and release calls. Release calls are important to both male and female, given the male's habit of jumping on just about anything that crosses his path, including floating apples, other males, and females of the wrong species. The release call, which has been described as a low-pitched chuckling sound, signals that a mistake has been made.

Amplexus, the scientific term for amphibian embrace, is a key reproductive behavior, even though only one Northwest amphibian, the tailed frog, actually copulates. Like a Heimlich maneuver gone awry, the male grips the female from above and squeezes her sides. When she's sufficiently prompted, both female and male make an external deposit of eggs and sperm. Clear jelly swells up around each fertilized egg.

The Pacific chorus frog is by far the most common and widespread frog in the Northwest. The delicate little creatures—two adults can fit on a business card—are green or brown and usually have a conspicuous black eye stripe. They have knobby toe pads adapted for climbing and can scale surfaces as smooth as glass. If you don't see any chorus frogs clinging to your patio door or the side of your house, check in tree branches and shrubs and on grasses and reeds.

While chorus frogs may be our most abundant species, tailed frogs are the most unique. Considered the most primitive living frog, tailed frogs are the only anuran that fertilizes eggs internally. "Tail" is a polite euphemism for the appendage that, while not a true penis, serves as the copulatory device. The tail can grow to an impressive proportion of the frog's overall length of one and a half to two inches. When mating, pairs may stay coupled for almost three days.

Further setting the species apart, tailed frogs are the only North American anuran specifically adapted for life in fast-flowing, cold forest streams. Tailed frogs were once considered rare, but experts now believe they can reach fairly high numbers in the right habitat. Put another way, they are as common as undisturbed forest streams.

For amphibian hunting with a regional flair, trail tailed-frog tadpoles to the quintessential Northwest habitat: clear, fast-flowing, year-round streams running through pristine forests. Explore streams in unlogged areas of the Gifford Pinchot Forest, or if you happen to find yourself in the North Cascades, check out Pyramid Creek, near Diablo off Highway 20 in the Ross Lake National Recreation Area. Keep an eye out for adults while you're at it, but they're hard to find because they have no voice—probably one more adaptation to living near loud, rushing water.

The best way to look for tailed-frog tadpoles is to pseudo-snorkel with a rigid, clear-plastic container like one you would use for storing leftovers. This type of container is usually carried by better kitchen-goods stores. When you've found a promising stream, find a shallow place near the bank where the water moves rapidly over smooth rocks, and press the container—upside-up, lid off, and submerged only halfway—against the frothy turbulence of the water's surface. The stream bottom will snap into refracted focus and open a viewing window into the water. Hold the plastic window box with one hand and use your other hand to gently turn over rocks and look for tadpoles glommed onto the rock bottoms. If your hand gets too cold before you've found your first tadpole, continue by browsing the rocks as they lie, watching for a fluttering, paper clip-sized tail protruding from crevices or rock piles.

Tailed-frog tadpoles use their teeth to hold fast to rocks and avoid being swept downstream by the current into some city's water supply. Should you manage to capture a tadpole with your small aquarium net, transfer it into your plastic box for a good view of its remarkable mouth. The oral disc, as it is called, has two to three rows of teeth in the upper "jaw" and eight to thirteen rows in the lower. The rows of teeth look like fine-toothed combs curved into a semicircle. Your hostage won't bite, even if you try to make it, but it will rasp along the plastic box in a hiccuping rhythm.

Northwest herpetologists believe that tailed frogs have the slowest development of any amphibian in the world, so the tadpole in your container may be three years old. There are laws against taking wildlife from the wild, so of course you'll want to release the tadpole back into its home stream.

When you get tired of kicking around for tadpoles and frogs, try turning up a salamander. Like tailed frogs, salamanders are harder to find because they are essentially voiceless. The Pacific giant salamander does make a growling noise, but only after you find it.

Salamanders are often confused with lizards, which are reptiles. Both animals have a basic chameleon shape, but reptiles have dry, scaly skin, claws on their toes, and are active during the day in hot, dry habitats. Salamanders, on the other hand, wouldn't be caught dead out at high noon. Or, actually, would be caught dead, because that's what they'd be. Dried up like raisins. Most salamanders look like they were pulled out of the oven before they were quite done. Their skin is necessarily thin and moist because they rely on their skin as much as their lungs for breathing, especially when hibernating underwater or in mud.

Larval salamanders look almost exactly like adults, except for the presence of external gills, which they wear like flying, feathery pigtails. Both adults and larvae can be found in the water, but only adults are ever found on land. We tend to think of salamanders—and other nocturnal animals—as rare, when all they may really be is overlooked.

During the day, adults like to hide under brush piles, debris piles, leaf litter, rocks, sheets of scrap tin, and the peeling bark of downed trees. Many salamanders prefer to be near water, but some of the woodland species, such as the ensatina and red-backed salamander, are often found in moist forests far from any body of water. You can peel back layers of bark, leaves, and rocks to look, without making it a search-and-destroy mission. Pat the layers back down the way you found them.

Look for juveniles in puddles, ponds, lakes, creeks, and streams. Fishermen occasionally hook the larvae of the Pacific giant salamander while casting for trout.

Rough-skinned newts are the exception to the nocturnal rule. Newts belong to a separate family within the salamander order and may be found in a wide variety of habitats, including forests, farmland, lakes, ponds, and streams. You might see them during the day swimming up to the surface of a lake for a gulp of air. The dark brown adult has sturdier-looking skin than other salamanders and may be more than six inches long.

Lacking the frog's ability to vocalize, salamanders have developed alternative ways of conducting courtship. Each species has a unique choreography of rubbing, nudging, and positioning that ensures no interspecies mating occurs. The result is a silent, secret, graceful ballet. Some species tangle in huge copulatory knots, although in the always modest Northwest, only rough-skinned newts gather in such a style.

Most salamanders in the Northwest progress from aquatic larva to terrestrial adult, although some remain in the gilled stage all their lives and are able to reproduce in this state. Neoteny, as it is known, can be tied both to species type and climatic factors.

The ability to respond to environmental factors is no doubt one of the reasons amphibians are one of our oldest life forms. But environmental changes may be coming too fast for the ancient ones to keep up with. Scientists are alarmed at the speed with which amphibians are disappearing. A conference led by the National Academy of Sciences in 1990 concluded that "drastic habitat modification is a major cause of the decline." Broadly considered, habitat modification includes acid rain and ozone depletion, as well as development, erosion, and the introduction of nonnative plants and animals.

Because of their permeable skin and the fact that their life cycle includes both water and soil, amphibians are particularly vulnerable to environmental contaminants. The fact that they eat insects, vessels of pesticide residue, further puts them at risk.

If you haven't caught a frog yet in your life, maybe you shouldn't wait too long.

tadpoles

Timing Your Visit: Amphibians can be found all summer in Gifford Pinchot National Forest. Frogs and toads may be most vocal in late spring and early summer.

Contact: For more information about the forest, contact Gifford Pinchot National Forest, 500 W. 12th Street, Vancouver, WA 98660; (206)750-5000.

For information on Northwest amphibians, contact the Washington Department of Wildlife Nongame Division, 600 Capitol Way N., Olympia, WA 98504; (206)753-5700. Or contact the Oregon Department of Fish and Wildlife Nongame Division, P.O. Box 59, Portland, OR 97207; (503)229-5403.

Getting There: To get to the South Prairie marsh in Gifford Pinchot National Forest from Vancouver, Washington, take Highway 14 east about 50 miles to the Cook–Willard turnoff. Follow the Cook–Underwood Road north about 5 miles and turn onto Willard Road. In a couple of miles, turn left onto South Prairie Road and drive about 13 miles to South Prairie marsh.

Accommodations: For information on area facilities, contact the Skamania County Chamber of Commerce, P.O. Box 1037D, Stevenson, WA 98648; (509)427-8911.

WHERE ELSE TO SEE AMPHIBIANS

WASHINGTON
Mount Baker National Recreation Area, northwestern Washington: The Heather Meadows area surrounding the final stretch of the Mount Baker Highway is a good place to look for frogs and salamanders in an alpine setting.

To get to the Mount Baker National Recreation Area from Bellingham, take Highway 542 east.

For more information on Heather Meadows, contact the Mount Baker–Snoqualmie National Forest, Glacier Ranger District Public Service Center, Glacier, WA 98244; (206)599-2714. For information on area facilities, contact the Mount Baker Foothills Chamber of Commerce, P.O. Box 5, Glacier, WA 98244; (206)599-2991.

Mount Rainier National Park, west-central Washington: Wet meadows off the Ricksecker Loop road and areas around Mount Rainier's lakes and streams are great places to look for amphibians.

To get to the Ricksecker Loop from the Nisqually entrance to Mount Rainier National Park, follow the road through Longmire and take the turnoff to Ricksecker Point.

For more information contact Mount Rainier National Park headquarters, Ashford, WA 98304; (206)569-2211. For information on area facilities, contact the Rainier/St. Helens Mountain Tourism Connections, P.O. Box 286DW, Ashford, WA 98304; (206)569-2628.

OREGON

Crater Lake National Park, southwestern Oregon: Long-toed salamanders, Pacific chorus frogs, and Cascade frogs are among the species that can be found in the area surrounding one of the world's deepest lakes. An amphibian checklist is available.

To get to Crater Lake National Park from Roseburg, take Highway 138 east to the park.

For more information about the park and its facilities, contact Crater Lake National Park Headquarters, P.O. Box 7, Crater Lake, OR 97604; (503)594-2211. For information on area facilities, contact the Klamath County Department of Tourism, P.O. Box 1867, Klamath Falls, OR 97601; (503)884-0666 or (800)445-6728.

Umatilla National Wildlife Refuge, northeastern Oregon: Located on the Columbia River, this refuge includes thousands of acres of ponds and marshes and several species of amphibians. Canoes and boats with electric motors are permitted.

To get to the Umatilla refuge from Pendleton, take Highway 84 to the Columbia River. The refuge is about 10 miles west of Umatilla on Highway 730.

For more information on Umatilla National Wildlife Refuge, contact refuge headquarters, P.O. Box 239, Umatilla, OR 97882; (503)922-3232. For information on area facilities, contact the Umatilla Chamber of Commerce, P.O. Box 59, Umatilla, OR 97882; (503)922-4825.

CHAPTER 8

A SPOT OF SUNLIGHT
Butterflies at Mima Mounds, Washington

*One day the Creator was watching some children playing in
a village. They laughed and sang, yet as he watched his heart
was sad. "These children will grow old," he thought. "Their
hair will turn gray. Their teeth will fall out. And those
wonderful flowers—yellow and blue, red and purple—will
fade. The leaves from the trees will fall and dry out."*

*He grew sadder and sadder. Thoughts of the coming
winter made his heart heavy. Yet it was still warm and the
sun was shining. The Creator watched the play of sun and
shadow on the ground; he saw the blue of the sky and the*

white of the cornmeal being ground by the women. Suddenly he smiled.

"All those colors ought to be preserved. I'll make something to gladden my heart, something for the children to look at and enjoy."

The Creator started gathering things: a spot of sunlight, handful of blue sky, white from the cornmeal, the shadow of a child, black from a little girl's hair, yellow from the falling leaves, and the reds, purples, and oranges of the flowers. All these he put into his bag. As an afterthought, he put in the songs of the birds.

"Children," he said, "this is for you." They opened the bag and a cloud of butterflies flew out fluttering and singing. The children listened, and laughed with joy.

But then a songbird landed on the Creator's shoulder and said, "It's not right to give our songs to your new playthings. Isn't it enough to have given them the colors of the rainbow?"

"You're right," said the Creator. "I shouldn't have taken what belongs to you." With that, he took song away from the butterflies and that's why they're silent today.

—Adapted from a Papago myth

Even without voices, butterflies harmonize summer days. From egg to caterpillar to chrysalis to butterfly—they create a visual melody line in the key of wonder.

Mima Mounds, near Olympia, is an enchanted place to look for an enchanting invertebrate. Footpaths wind through fields of hillocks up to eight feet tall and fifty feet around, frosted with wildflowers, mosses, and ferns. Small stands of fir and pine are scattered among the mounds like kiosk-forests. Rarely crowded, the place seems suspended from reality and is only occasionally disturbed by the cracks and zings from a far-off rifle range or the buzzing of model airplanes somewhere to the south.

From the air, Mima Mounds looks like the earth with a serious case of goose bumps. The mounded topography was extensive before twentieth-century civilization leveled huge sections for development. Nineteenth-century artist Paul Kane, who did paintings of the mounds, wrote that he traveled through twenty-two miles of the curious landscape. Today, 470 acres of the remaining prairie are protected by the Washington Department of Natural Resources as a natural preserve.

Mima Mounds isn't the only place on earth where these crowded humps exist, but it is the definitive place. Whether in the Andes or California, similar formations are referred to as "Mima mounds."

While there are no sure explanations of how the mounds came to be, there are plenty of ideas. The burial-mound hypothesis has been abandoned because Mima has little significance in local Native American culture and no artifacts have ever been discovered there. The remaining theories fall into three main categories: frost or ice erosion, earthquakes, and gophers. Not giant gophers, either—just plain old pocket gophers. The gopher theory was advanced by respected biologists Victor B. Scheffer and Walter W. Dahlquest and remains one of the more plausible postulations.

Arthur R. Kruckeberg's *The Natural History of Puget Sound Country* offers a thorough account of several Mima origin hypotheses and discusses the area's geography in detail. What we do know is that Mima Prairie is a natural, nonforested plain with the concomitant sunshine and flowers that go along with open space. It is east-side habitat on the west side of the Cascade Range. This fact has not been lost on the butterflies, making Mima Mounds one of Washington's best places to butterfly in the lowlands west of the Cascade crest. Ochre ringlets, silvery blues, anise swallowtails, and Sara's orange-tips are just some of the species that levitate over Mima's buttercups, violets, camas lilies, shooting stars, dandelions, oxeye daisies, and other weeds and wildflowers.

While Mima is indeed a fascinating spot, you can find butterflies just about anywhere there are flowers, sunshine, and a bit of open space. Keep in mind that flowers aren't the only draw for butterflies. Some species are also quite fond of animal excrement and carrion for the amino acids those substances provide. Butterflies are also drawn to mud puddles, where they can extract minerals from salts in damp soil or sand. Rotting fruit—another favorite—can even be used for butterfly baiting. A ripe banana mashed with stale wine, or beer mixed with honey or sugar and poured over a sandy spot can really bring them in.

Other promising places to see butterflies are unsprayed power-line rights-of-way, vacant lots, pastures, parks, and unsprayed roadsides. Vineyards can also be delightful butterflying destinations, especially when coupled with some nectar sipping of your own. If you create your own garden with plants that attract butterflies, you won't have to go anywhere. Inspire yourself with a good book on butterfly gardening.

Butterfly watching is a civilized pursuit. Forget the early mornings, late twilights, swamps, and caves of bats and toads; butterflying is best in the midday sunshine. If it's not sunny, go to a movie. A few butterflies may be out on cloudy days, but they're the exceptions.

The pastime requires very little beyond a field guide and sun hat, but if you think you may really get into it, buy or make a butterfly net. A butterfly can be held and released without harm if you hold it gently but firmly just above the thorax (the part of the body where the legs and wings are attached) so that all four wings are held closed. Blunt-ended stamp tweezers are a good tool for this and may be less clumsy than your fingers. If you do catch butterflies, you will want a hand lens to study the iridescent scales, antennae, compound eyes, and proboscis, or tube tongue, which coils against the butterfly's chin.

proboscis

I ordered some caterpillars from an insect supply house and was most impressed with the way each emerging painted lady limbered up its proboscis—flinging and drawing it back like a yo-yo. They could do "sleeper," "walk-the-dog," and "around-the-world."

Butterflies and moths share the order Lepidoptera, from the Greek words *lepis* for "scale" and *ptera* for "wing," a reference to the tiny scales that shingle butterfly wings like shavings off a precious jewel. Some scales get their color from reflective pigment; others have a prismatic structure and take their color from refracted sunlight. Blues, greens, golds, and silvers are usually refracted light; yellows, whites, browns, blacks, and reds are most often pigment-based. The scales brush off relatively easily—they are the fairy dust left on your fingers after you touch a butterfly. A moderate loss of scales doesn't seem to hurt the wing or affect the butterfly's ability to fly.

Of the 20,000 or so butterfly species identified worldwide, some 700 occur in North America. About 200 are native to the Northwest. Don't be daunted by the numbers; there are workable ways to sort them out. Butterflies fall into two distinct superfamilies: the true butterflies (Papilionoidea) and the skippers (Hesperioidea). Generally, the true butterflies have slender bodies and broad wings and fly with fluttery wingbeats. Heads are proportionately small, and the antennae are close together at the base. By comparison, skippers have stouter bodies with short, strong-looking wings and antennae set far apart on a big head. They take the name "skipper" from their swift, erratic flight and brisk, blurred wingbeats.

Skippers, especially the big, furry ones, can resemble moths. Although no butterflies fly at night, some moths do fly during the day; so the best way to tell skipper from moth is by the antennae. Both true butterfly and skipper antennae are always knobbed, though the knobbing is sometimes subtle. Outside the tropics, moth antennae, which can be feathery or smooth, are never knobbed.

Within the true butterfly and skipper superfamilies are groups whose members share distinctive characteristics. With a little practice, even a novice can identify parnassians, coppers, sulfurs, hairstreaks, fritillaries, checkerspots, anglewings, swallowtails, blues, and so on.

Before heading afield, peruse a butterfly field guide to get a feel for the different groups. Many guides are available, although the *Audubon Society Field Guide to North American Butterflies,* with its color photographs and thumb tab key, is particularly informative and easy to use.

Color, pattern, size, wing shape, and behavior are among the principal clues for identification. For instance, tiger swallowtails have lobed tails and are yellow with black bands; whites and sulphurs are white or yellow and are the butterflies we often see along roadsides. What's today's date? Butterflies have recognized flight periods—times of year that they most commonly appear—so the calendar date can also be important. One of the first butterflies you may see in the spring is the mourning cloak, a chocolate brown beauty with a glycol-like substance in its blood that serves as antifreeze. The mourning cloak actually hibernates as a fully formed adult.

Skippers tend to be dark and often sit with their triangular wings spread flat. Wood nymphs are also dark but have conspicuous eye spots. Hairstreaks will have hairlike tails on their hind wings; blues and coppers are usually metallic or iridescent. Anglewings have the look of a tomcat's tattered ear.

Are the wings hooked, rounded, or triangular? Checked, spotted, or solid? And off you go.

The average life span of most butterflies is only about two weeks, so it's no wonder they're obsessed with the task of reproduction. In his *Handbook for Butterfly Watchers,* noted butterfly expert and author Robert Michael Pyle writes, "The ultimate purpose of butterflies is to make more of the same and the ultimate in butterfly behavior, from both the watcher's and the butterfly's perspectives, is courtship and coupling."

Noting the behavior of common and orange sulphurs, Pyle observes, "If two males come into contact, they will likely orbit one another upward for a time, then, realizing their error, disengage and plummet in opposite directions. An encounter between a male and an unreceptive female may eventuate similarly. But if a male and a receptive female engage, the spiral flight goes on and on. Eventually the pair drops to the ground, where they begin a terrestrial dance in the aftermath of the aerial minuet already performed."

The dance is lovely, but pheromones are the final whammy. Pheromones are special chemical scents strong enough to be detected even by a human nose at close range. These fragrances are unique to each species. The distinct scents both attract members of the opposite sex and help ensure against interspecies breeding. Butterflies detect pheromones through their antennae, which would more accurately be nicknamed "sniffers" instead of "feelers."

If butterflies are mating machines, caterpillars are eating machines, beginning from the time they bite their way out of their eggs. Over a month or two, the munching marauders increase their weight up to ten-thousandfold. Some caterpillars molt several times in order to accommodate this growth; each period between molts is called an instar. What comes next is worth the sacrifice of a few leaves: the remarkable transformation from caterpillar to butterfly.

Caterpillars form chrysalides at this pupal stage. Both moths and butterflies make chrysalides, but many moths go on to spin covering cocoons. Chrysalides take many shapes, such as curled leaves, thorns, pellets, or pods. Within the chrysalis, the caterpillar relaxes its form into organic soupiness and then slowly rearranges itself into a butterfly. Some species spend as little as eight days in the pupal stage, but others may spend years in the chrysalis. Swallowtails are among the species that overwinter in chrysalides.

chrysalis

I watched my four fat, mail-order caterpillars form shells in which they hung from the lid of their plastic container like upside-down monks. Golden spots decorated the mysterious casings and every once in a while a chrysalis would shiver with the work going on inside.

You don't have to buy caterpillars to observe metamorphosis. Just look around your neighborhood for eggs or caterpillars to raise. Many butterfly field guides include descriptions of eggs and caterpillars and also list host plants. Two-thirds of North American butterfly species will eat only one plant or family of plants—one of the reasons loss of habitat and the disappearance of native plants can be so devastating to butterfly populations.

Store-bought caterpillars come with a layer of "nutrient" in the bottom of the container, so feeding them isn't a problem. But raising caterpillars you catch requires procuring continuous fresh supplies of the preferred food plant. Picking caterpillars from plants they're eating in your own yard is ideal. Containers need not be elaborate; a screened shoebox or mayonnaise jar will suffice as long as it's kept out of direct sunlight and has fresh air, fresh food, and a few sticks or leaves to accommodate a hanging chrysalis. *Peterson's Field Guide to Western Butterflies* has a brief but good discussion on raising butterflies.

Several Lepidoptera species have become extinct within the last century, and species that were once common are getting harder to find. As noted butterfly photographer Kjell B. Sandved said, "If even one of the lowly species of butterflies becomes extinct, a new heaven and a new earth must come to pass to create it again."

One Northwest butterfly, the Oregon silverspot, is on the federal government's list of threatened species and is also on Washington's threatened list. Oregon doesn't list insects. The medium-size, orange-and-brown Oregon silverspot was once found all along the Washington and Oregon coasts in salt-spray meadows. This fragile coastal ecosystem has been all but eliminated by recreational vehicles and development; weeds and rough grasses have pushed out native violets, which silverspot caterpillars depended upon for food. It's possible that the Oregon silverspot has dwindled beyond recovery within the last few years. We should add a third category—ecosystems—to the federal government's threatened and endangered list.

Aristotle used the word *psyche* to mean both "soul" and "butterfly." Indeed, ancient Greeks believed that the soul left the body in the form of a butterfly. Maybe butterflies can give a body back its soul too. Slow down. Settle into the flowers and let the Creator's playthings come to you. Be patient. See the white of the cornmeal, the black of a little girl's hair, the blue of the sky. Adjust to the stillness and listen for the lost butterfly voices.

Timing Your Visit: Butterflies are flying all summer at Mima Mounds. Weather is the most important consideration; butterfly watching is good on just about any sunny day.

Contact: For more information on Mima Mounds, contact the Washington Department of Natural Resources, Public Lands Building, Olympia, WA 98504; (206)753-5327.

Caterpillars can be ordered through Insect Lore Products, P.O. Box 1535, Shafter, CA 93263; (800)LIVE BUG.

Getting There: To get to Mima Mounds from Olympia, take I-5 south about 10 miles to the Highway 121 exit and go west about 3 miles to Littlerock. At Littlerock, go straight instead of following Highway 121. When the road ends at a T, go right and then bear left on Waddell Creek Road. The Mima Mounds entrance is just ahead on your left; watch for the sign.

Accommodations: For information on area facilities, contact the Thurston County Chamber of Commerce, P.O. Box 1427, Olympia, WA 98507; (206)357-3362.

WHERE ELSE TO SEE BUTTERFLIES

WASHINGTON

L. T. Murray Wildlife Area, central Washington: More than sixty species of butterflies flutter over 103,000 acres of prolific wildflowers, rangeland, and stands of ponderosa pine.

To get to L. T. Murray from Ellensburg, take Umtanum Road south.

For more information on L. T. Murray Wildlife Area, contact the Washington Department of Wildlife Regional Office, 2802 Fruitvale Boulevard, Yakima, WA 98902; (509)575-2740. For information on area facilities, contact the Ellensburg Chamber of Commerce, 436 N. Sprague Street, Ellensburg, WA 98926; (509)925-3137.

Mount Rainier National Park, west-central Washington: Checkered whites, Milbert's tortoiseshells, coppers, blues, and alpines are among the butterflies you may see flitting over highmountain wildflower meadows around the Mount Rainier village of Paradise.

To get to Paradise from Seattle, take I-5 south to the Highway 161 exit to Puyallup. Take Highway 161 to Highway 7 and then join Highway 706, the Mount Rainier loop road.

For more information on Mount Rainier National Park, contact park headquarters, Ashford, WA 98304; (206)569-2211. For information on area facilities, contact the Rainier/St. Helens Mountain Tourism Connection, P.O. Box 286DW, Ashford, WA 98304; (206)569-2628.

OREGON

Moon Point Special Interest Area, western Oregon: This special area within the Willamette National Forest includes wetlands, wildflower meadows, and cliffs—all good butterfly habitats. A 1-mile trail takes you to the old Moon Point fire lookout.

To get to Moon Point from Eugene, take I-5 south and exit

to Highway 58. Go east past Oakridge, turn south on Kitson Springs Road, right on Forest Road 21, left on Forest Road 2129, and right on Forest Road 2129-439. It's a long, twisty road; carry a good map.

For maps and more information on the Moon Point Special Interest Area, contact the Rigdon Ranger District, 49098 Salmon Creek Road, Oakridge, OR 97463; (503)782-2283. For information on facilities, contact the Oakridge Chamber of Commerce, P.O. Box 217, Oakridge, OR 97463; (503)782-4146.

Steens Mountain Scenic Loop, southeastern Oregon: Butterflies make their own sparkling current over barely wet creek beds and throng roadside plants in the high desert of Steens Mountain. The loop road is a Bureau of Land Management Scenic Back Road Byway.

To get to Steens Mountain from Bend, take Highway 20 east to Burns and go south on Highway 205. Pick up the loop road in Frenchglen or farther down Highway 205.

For more information on Steens Mountain Scenic Loop, contact the Bureau of Land Management District Office, HC 74-12533 Highway 20 W., Hines, OR 97738; (503)573-5241. For information on area facilities, contact the Harney County Chamber of Commerce, 18 West D Street, Burns, OR 97720; (503)573-2636.

CHAPTER 9

PELICANS IN POTHOLES

White Pelicans at Potholes Reservoir, Washington

Later, Joan confessed that at first she thought we were overdoing it. But Ron said to sneak, so we sneaked. Turning our backs on the sage plain, the three of us entered the oasis of green bordering the north end of Potholes Reservoir near Moses Lake. Single file, no talking, we stroked through curtains of willow and held our breath through rustling, hip-high grass.

We bunched at the base of a six-foot embankment, nodded to one another, and crawled up through the bushes to peek down the other side. Standing about seventy-five yards away on the opposite shore of the shallow pothole, 200 white pelicans carried on unaware. The birds milled about amiably, beaks pressed in hairpin curves against their long necks. Waddling with a bit of a swagger, they clacked their beaks in occasional commentary. The adults stood about three feet tall and were all white, except for ink-black wing tips and yellow-orange bills. Juveniles were distinguishable by their gray caps and dusky bills.

As we watched, about twenty took to the water, transforming the scene into a fluttering *Fantasia*. The feathery white half-moons swam forward in a gang, beating the water with their black wing tips, which they had folded out like steel from a switchblade.

On a hidden cue they began tipping forward, dipping their heads in and out of the water in rolling syncopation, stitching up mouthfuls of the little fish that had crowded before their churning wings. The birds turned in unison, working along the shoreline in ruffly grace. Soft bathing sounds came muffled across the still air. Sage smells carried on the heat, and bugs buzzed heavily through our hide-out.

Having had its fill, one bird split off and started swimming back toward shore. Several fell in behind like loose electrons. A short-sided V of airborne pelicans spiraled down on nine-foot wingspans to join the others, rustling the air as they funneled over us. Stunningly graceful, they held in silent formation—heads pulled back, beaks on necks, feet tucked in, wing tips skinning the air.

My legs had been asleep for twenty minutes when Ron gave the signal to go. After twenty years as a wildlife biologist in central Washington, he finds as much pleasure sneaking away from the flighty birds as he does sneaking up on them. We crept away, left speechless by the spectacle anyway.

For anyone not familiar with the inland landscape, the notion of pelicans in central Washington may seem odd. Pelicans are brown and belong at the beach, right? They stand on piers and appear on postcards from Florida, Mexico, and California. But there are such things as white pelicans that do live hundreds of miles from the nearest salt water. In fact, white pelicans have been part of the interior ecosystem for 40 million years.

The history of pelicans in the Moses Lake area is sketchy, but records indicate that there may have been about two dozen nesting pairs in the early to mid-1920s. At that time, Potholes

Reservoir wasn't even a pipe dream. It was in the 1950s that the Columbia River Reclamation irrigation project put pipe to the dream and delivered water unto the desert. Agricultural land rolled its green carpet over gray-brown shrub-steppe, towns grew around farms, and Potholes Reservoir spread over thousands of acres.

Before the area was flooded by the project, sand dunes had marched across the broad basin. When O'Sullivan Dam was built to create Potholes Reservoir, water backed up over an expanse of dunes; most of the small islands you see scattered in the reservoir are their crests. Shifting dunes are still visible to the east and west of the reservoir.

Irrigation wasn't the first water to flood that country. About 16,000 years ago, the ice dam that formed Glacial Lake Missoula broke, letting loose 500 cubic *miles* of water that roared from Montana all the way past Moses Lake. Geologists figure the wall of water was 2,000 feet high. The same glacial lake is thought to have filled and flooded from twenty-five to forty times, smashing, pushing, scouring, and rearranging every natural feature in its path. To this day, these Spokane Floods, as they're called, hold the record in the geologic book of cataclysm.

Even though the irrigation project seems tame in comparison, the Columbia River Reclamation project changed local ecology significantly. Less than 100 years ago, the Columbia River Basin was almost entirely shrub-steppe—a dry, but very much alive, habitat characterized by a variety of grasses, sages, and other shrubs, and home to an interesting and abundant mix of birds, reptiles, and mammals. Today, only about half of the original habitat remains. Many of the indigenous animal species, including sage grouse, sharptail grouse, pygmy rabbits, burrowing owls, and striped whipsnakes, were displaced as their native land was transformed by borrowed water for agricultural, residential, and recreational uses. On the bright side, the numbers of ducks and geese have grown steadily since the reservoir was established. And although the area is no longer suitable for nesting pelicans because of the disturbance factor, the Potholes, with all its water and fish, is probably a more productive migratory stopover now for pelicans than it was before.

O'Sullivan Dam is located on the south end of the reservoir. I don't particularly like dams, but I have to confess that I love driving over them. O'Sullivan Dam cuts an end-of-the-world edge. On one side, the reservoir stretches wet and sparkling into the distance. Ski boats leave white trails, motorhomes are parked along the beach, and everything looks busy and twentieth century. On the other side, well below the road and the water level, the land is an eroded complex of strip-woven, dry streambeds that looks like sculpted time. Channeled scablands. The name is descriptive, but too unlovely for such striking terrain.

Just past the east end of the dam, loons were paddling in the reservoir near the shore. We stopped to watch and wondered if they had been around B.P.—Before Potholes. After a steady history of habitat alteration, from dryland farming and ranching to irrigated agriculture, it's tricky to know which plants and animals have always belonged.

Some newcomers are welcome. The more ducks the merrier. But not all nonindigenous species are benign. An ornamental plant called purple loosestrife is one of the reservoir's most insidious invaders. The waving purple patches visible around the Potholes look beautiful until you know that they kill wetlands. Originally introduced from Europe, purple—and now a new strain of yellow—loosestrife squeezes out native vegetation and offers nothing in return. Birds don't eat the seeds, muskrats don't use the stalks to build houses, stands of loosestrife are too dense to use as cover, and the weed spreads to fill in open water, eliminating habitat for pelicans, ducks, and other waterfowl. Loosestrife looks somewhat like fireweed and Douglas spirea and had been sold in Washington nurseries as an ornamental until its sale in the state was banned. Efforts are under way to control loosestrife, but the battle will be monumental and expensive. You can help by not picking and transporting any pretty, spiky, purple flowers.

Fortunately, there is still plenty of open water to entice white pelicans to stop over on their way to and from Canadian breeding grounds. The birds arrive at the Potholes in March and April sporting a tablike appendage halfway down the upper portion of their beaks, or mandibles. These tabs, which look like mini centerboards, are part of the breeding plumage and will drop off later in the season.

Only a few pelicans remain in Washington for the whole

summer; these are probably birds under three years old that are not yet reproducing. The majority press on north without too much delay. The pelicans we see at the Potholes are thought to be members of a colony that nests in south-central British Columbia near Williams Lake. Most of North America's 150,000 white pelicans nest in central Canada, primarily Manitoba.

In the far western United States the number of breeding colonies has fallen from about twenty-three to five; two in Oregon, two in California, and one in Nevada. Today the colonies are fairly stable and, in some cases, even building. About a dozen others are scattered across the country from Montana to Minnesota and down into Texas.

Pelicans return to the Potholes in late summer, lingering a little longer than they did in the spring. The birds fatten up for the fall migration and mark the skies with a presence evocatively prehistoric. Numbers are at their peak in late July and August. In most years the count averages a few hundred birds, but in 1990 more than 1,600 pelicans were in the greater Potholes area in late August. Biologists speculate that the birds had been starved out of home territories in California and Nevada because of drought.

Although brown pelicans are on the federal government's list of threatened and endangered species, white pelicans are not. They are, however, on Washington's list of endangered species and on Oregon's list of sensitive species. The pesticide DDT had a less disastrous impact on white pelicans than on browns, although the effect was still severe. But even before DDT, white pelicans had faced other threats.

Around the turn of the century, plume collectors took a terrible toll on all birds with beautiful feathers, including pelicans. Herons, especially, were slaughtered in unconscionable numbers. Early conservationists estimated that nearly 193,000 herons had been killed to provide the feathers for a single London auction house during 1902. Extensive public-awareness campaigns eventually led to protective legislation, and the feather trade died off. Use of the egret as a symbol of the bird preservation movement sprang from those campaigns. Also around the turn of the century, commercial fishermen lobbied successfully to exclude pelicans from the Migratory Bird Treaty between the United States and Canada. Believing pelicans competed for fish resources, fishermen destroyed large numbers of birds and eggs.

A more current threat to white pelicans comes from tourists, bird watchers, and researchers who approach breeding colonies too closely during critical nesting times. Some biologists say that approaching a breeding colony is tantamount to killing several young birds. It's best to view pelicans away from nesting areas in places such as the Potholes, where birds aren't in such a vulnerable state. As long as the pelicans aren't made to fly and are allowed to maintain access to food and cover, disturbance is minimal.

Pelicans eat three to four pounds of fish a day. Brown pelicans plunge straight into the ocean from high in the sky to catch their fish, but white pelicans would have broken their last neck ages ago using the same strategy in shallow lakes.

As we had witnessed from our brushy hide-out, white pelicans often hunt cooperatively, herding prey into shallow water and then rocking forward to scoop up the fish. Pelicans don't tip radically like dabbling ducks, who turn bottom up to feed in the mud—theirs is a more moderate, graceful motion.

The pelican's famous pouch is formed by an elastic membrane that rims the lower mandible and connects to the bird's neck. When the pouch is full, the mandible can bow out like those oval, rubber change purses drugstores used to give away. The gular membrane, as it is technically known, is covered by a network of blood vessels and is also important in respiration. When the pelican is hot, it can flutter the membrane to cool itself down.

Pelicans don't fly with fish in their pouches because it would make them front-heavy. When carrying food to their young, they swallow the fish to later regurgitate at the chick's urging. The parent opens its mouth, exposing its gullet, and the young bird pecks around, often putting its head completely into the parent's mouth until some food is disgorged.

Pelicans are monogamous, and both male and female participate in incubating the eggs and feeding the young. Two eggs are typically laid.

Before it leaves the nest, the largest chick will probably kill, or at least cause the death of, its younger nestmate. Many biologists say this apparent siblicide is nature's way of seeing that the number of chicks matches the abundance of food. However, others counter that the larger chick kills the smaller even in times of plenty. This latter contingent believes the second egg is insurance against losing the first to predators or other environmental pressures. It could be, they reason, that pelican parents never intend or expect to raise two young. They base their hypothesis on incubation style. Some birds delay incubation until all eggs have been laid so that they will hatch at once. But others, including the pelican, begin to incubate an egg as soon as it is laid. One egg may hatch several days before the other, giving the first chick a jump on the second.

In any case, the surviving chick is well attended. After spending two to three weeks in a simple nest scraped into the ground, chicks band together with other juveniles in pods. From then until they fledge (learn to fly), chicks remain in the pods, where their beleaguered parents continue to serve them. The loud, demanding youngsters gain as much as twenty pounds before their first flight, often coming to outweigh the adults by several pounds. The extra fat will be spent while the chick is learning to fly and hunt for itself.

By the time the pelicans come down to the Potholes to loaf and fish and finish out the summer, the only visible difference between juvenile and adult is the immature bird's grayish cap and bill.

Some pelicans stay at the Potholes until October, when they continue south to the Gulf states and Mexico. The best time to see them depends more on water level than on numbers of birds. Lower water levels concentrate fish and also reduce the number of boats taking up the territory. The best place to see them, says Ron, is "where it's hard for people to get to."

The northwestern corner of the reservoir is used by pelicans fairly consistently, and they are also seen in the reservoir's southeastern corner by the east arm of Lind Coulee and in Frenchman Hills Lake, west of south Potholes. If you look in all these places and still don't find any pelicans, it's time to invoke Edward Lear's "The Pelican Chorus." You can practice on your way over to the Potholes. It works every time, if you really believe. Ready?

King and Queen of the Pelicans we;
No other birds so grand we see!

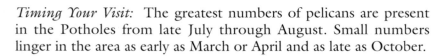

None but we have feet like fins!
With lovely leathery throats and chins!

Ploffskin, Pluffskin, Pelican jee!
We think no birds so happy as we!
Plumpskin, Plashkin, Pelican jill!
We think so then, and we thought so still!

Timing Your Visit: The greatest numbers of pelicans are present in the Potholes from late July through August. Small numbers linger in the area as early as March or April and as late as October.

Contact: For more information about Potholes Reservoir, contact the Washington Department of Wildlife, 1540 Alder Street, N.W., Ephrata, WA 98823; (509)754-4624.

Getting There: To get to Potholes Reservoir from Ellensburg, drive east on I-90 to Moses Lake, about 72 miles. To get to the north end of the reservoir from Moses Lake, drive about 3½ miles west on the I-90 frontage road and turn left onto the north Potholes access road.

To get to Frenchman Hills Lake and Lind Coulee (both on the south side of the reservoir) from I-90, either take Dodson Road off I-90 about 12 miles west of Moses Lake, or take Highway 17 south, just east of Moses Lake.

Accommodations: For information on area facilities, contact the Moses Lake Area Chamber of Commerce, 324 S. Pioneer Way, Moses Lake, WA 98837; (509)765-7888.

WHERE ELSE TO SEE WHITE PELICANS

WASHINGTON
Umatilla National Wildlife Refuge, Washington Unit, south-central Washington: This refuge stretches about 18 miles along the Columbia River. Half is in Washington and half in Oregon. Paterson Slough, east of Paterson, is a productive bird-watching site.

To get to the Washington side of the Umatilla refuge from the

Tri-Cities of Kennewick, Pasco, and Richland, take I-82 south and then take Highway 14 west toward Paterson and look for the slough.

For more information on the refuge, contact the Umatilla National Wildlife Refuge, P.O. Box 239, Umatilla, OR 97882; (503)922-3232. For information on area facilities, contact the Tri-Cities Visitor Bureau, P.O. Box 2241, Tri-Cities, WA 99302; (509)735-8486.

McNary National Wildlife Refuge, southeastern Washington: Located 6 miles south of Pasco off Highway 12, the McNary refuge is situated near the confluence of the Columbia and Snake rivers. A 1-mile nature trail circles the slough area. The Washington Department of Wildlife manages a separate section, the McNary Habitat Management Area, on the other side of Highway 12. Check both for pelicans.

To get to McNary National Wildlife Refuge from Pasco, take Highway 12 west to the refuge, which begins on the other side of the Snake River.

For more information about McNary National Wildlife Refuge, contact refuge headquarters, P.O. Box 308, Burbank, WA 99323; (509)547-4942. For information on area facilities, contact the Tri-Cities Visitor Bureau, P.O. Box 2241, Tri-Cities, WA 99302; (509)735-8486.

OREGON
Malheur National Wildlife Refuge, southeastern Oregon: Located in the southeastern corner of Oregon, Malheur Lake is a primary stop for migrating white pelicans. Pelicans are sometimes visible from refuge headquarters.

To get to Malheur National Wildlife Refuge headquarters from Burns, take Highway 205 south, and in about 25 miles turn east on the county road toward Princeton and drive about 9 miles.

For more information on Malheur National Wildlife Refuge, contact refuge headquarters, HC-72 Box 245, Princeton, OR 97721; (503)493-2612. For information on area facilities, contact the Harney County Chamber of Commerce, 18 West D Street, Burns, OR 97720; (503)573-2636.

Lower Klamath National Wildlife Refuge, south-central Oregon: Pelicans linger in the Lower Klamath refuge through the summer and can be seen on the self-guided driving tour.

To get to the refuge from Klamath Falls, drive south on Highway 97 about 19 miles. Turn east into the refuge on Highway 161, which runs along the California–Oregon border. To get to refuge headquarters, located east of the refuge in California, turn south off Highway 161 onto Hill Road and go about 4 miles.

For the latest viewing information and driving tour brochure, contact the Klamath Basin National Wildlife Refuges, Route 1, Box 74, Tulelake, CA 96134; (916)667-2231. For information on area facilities, contact the Klamath County Department of Tourism, P.O. Box 1867, Klamath Falls, OR 97601; (800)445-6728.

CHAPTER 10

HOW LOW CAN YOU GO?

Solstice Tidepooling at Rosario Beach, Washington

Poseidon was having a summer open house. He has one every year around the solstice when daytime tides draw the sea back to one of its lowest points of the year. It was a lavish affair, with some of his most exquisite treasures on display. Tiny snails filled a large, empty barnacle shell like pearls in a goblet. Splashes of living color adorned rocks in bright abstractions. Tidepools were set about like aquariums for the guests' enjoyment.

I paused at one, as big as a big man's shoe, and counted thirty-five anemones, five hermit crabs, a tidepool sculpin, four limpets, a knot of ribbon worms, and one urchin—all very small, all very busy, all very beautiful.

Tidepools form on rocky shores within a sash of earth claimed by both land and sea. Rosario Beach, near Washington's Deception Pass State Park, is one such sash, gloriously decorated with shifting, swaying rickrack.

The summer solstice, longest day of the year and official beginning of summer, falls on June 20 or 21 in this part of the world. The lowest tide may not be precisely on that date, but it will be close. The winter solstice also has extremely low tides, but it's cold and dark; so I celebrate summer by tidepooling and settle for a bonfire in December.

As I walked farther over the rocks toward the retreating sea, little pillows of rockweed popped and wheezed under my feet. The foamy substance inside the green-yellow plant is said to be antiseptic and astringent. I rubbed some on my skin where barnacles had scraped my elbows. You need to get your nose right down over the tidepool to take everything in, which can put you on all fours among the rough barnacles and slippery seaweeds.

I found another tidepool, this one the size of a washtub, and hunkered down. Activity paused while I settled my shadow over the water, but the cast of creatures quickly reemerged. Hermit crabs no bigger than a fingernail took center stage. Arms flailing, the obsessive janitors swept across the tidepool floor consuming decayed material. In another corner, seaweed shifted as a purple shore crab peered out and then resumed eating its sea lettuce cover. A marble-sized crystal ball steadily propelled itself across tidepool space—a comb jelly, or "sea gooseberry."

After a while of leaning over the still pool, the surface disappeared. From the shadows, an eel-like gunnel fish dashed out to snatch a mouthful of zooplankton.

The word *plankton* comes from the Greek *planktos*, meaning "to wander." Zooplankton (small drifting animals) and phytoplankton (small drifting plants) steady the base of the food chain so that we can stand at the top. Phytoplankton is also responsible for producing a substantial portion of the earth's oxygen.

Zooplankton includes both fully developed organisms and the larvae of animals that will eventually grow large. (The term *larvae* is used to describe the early stages of an organism that changes substantially from juvenile to adult. Tadpoles are larval frogs, for instance.) Shrimp, crabs, snails, octopi, and sea urchins all spend part of their lives as zooplankton. Under a hand lens, you can see the minuscule animals tear around at top speed like there's no tomorrow, which, for many of them, is precisely the case. A friend calls them "zoomplankton."

Nearly everything is something in a tidepool. That yellowish, inch-long bit of feathery flotsam is a barnacle's molted inner casing. Those roundish decals on the kelp are bryozoa, complex colonies of microscopic animals.

barnacles

I blink and a cone-shaped limpet slowly glides across a rock under the water, shell slightly lifted, antennae waving languidly. It leaves a light-colored trail, evidence of a radula at work. Limpets and other algae-eating mollusks, such as abalone and nudibranches, use their abrasive tongues, called radulae, to scrape food off the rocks.

The distribution of organisms in the intertidal region between high and low tide has been carefully thought out. Rocky shore-lines can have up to four distinct zones. Plants and animals develop special adaptations for their home zones, although zones and the creatures in them can blend into one another. Rosario Beach is special in that the four zones are easily recognizable.

The uppermost level—the splash zone—is constantly moist-ened by ocean spray but is under water only at extreme high tides. In the splash zone, lichen, moss, and algae spread a welcome mat at the door of the next zone down.

The high-tide zone, uncovered during most of a twenty-four-hour day, is home to mostly hard-shelled creatures such as acorn barnacles, finger limpets, and shore crabs.

Things begin to look Dr. Seuss-ish in the mid-tide zone. Increased submersion time results in more variety of marine species, and because the wave action is less fierce, animals here can get along without a hard shell. Globby anemones and plump sea stars first appear here, but not all residents are shell-less. Gumboot chitons move slowly back and forth between this zone and the next like glacial meatloaves.

The largest species of chiton on earth, gumboots grow up to a foot long and curl up like perturbed armadillos if pried off their home rock (*not* a nice thing to do). When they die, chitons leave behind eight butterfly-shaped shell segments—treasured by beachcombers as highly as sand dollars.

In the fourth zone—the low-tide zone—bottom-dwellers are exposed only about twice a month. This bohemian community includes nudibranches, sponges, and sea cucumbers, along with increasingly outrageous species of sea stars and anemones.

Anemones are the image many people conjure up when they think of a tidepool. The "elegant anemone," one of the most common Northwest species, is subdued green with delicate-pink tentacles. Blossomed out in the pool, elegant anemones look like fluffy marine wild roses. When low tides leave them uncovered, anemones close up and hunker in the rocks like clusters of strange overripe fruit.

Anemones, along with jellyfish and sea pens, belong to the phylum Cnidaria, from the Greek word for "nettle." All cnidaria have stinging cells, although nettles will give you a far greater sting than most of the cnidarians you're likely to run into in a tidepool.

While some anemone species reproduce sexually, many, including the elegant one, clone themselves. All the individuals in this tightly bunched colony under my nose had likely originated from a single parent that divided itself over and over to create a batch of genetically identical organisms. When one xenophobic clone cluster encroaches upon the territory of another, war breaks out. Anemones on both front lines shoot stinging cells at each other until a no-anemone-land is formed.

The stinging cells are trouble for other intertidal neighbors as well. Although anemones are sometimes called "sea flowers," "sea warriors" would be more accurate. The innocuous-looking animals are aggressive carnivores that use their tentacles to capture small crustaceans and zooplankton to eat—a good reminder that not all predators are warm-blooded vertebrates with big teeth. The chase is slower in a tidepool but no less final.

Sea stars are among the most predatory of invertebrates, hunting clams, barnacles, chitons, mussels, and just about anything else that can't outcreep them. The sea star slides over its prey and gets a grip on the victim's shell with its rows of suction-cuplike tube feet. With a steady pull, it opens the shell and pushes part of its stomach into the crack to digest the contents.

And they're so cute when they're little—like tiny, bright asterisks sticking onto the dark rocks. The six-rayed sea star, one of our most common intertidal stars, is especially attentive to its little ones. Between December and March, adults of both sexes congregate under rocks in groups of a dozen or so and cast their spawning ingredients at more or less the same time—the females releasing eggs from the pores on their backs. A female will catch any fertilized eggs that haven't drifted away and hold them in a cluster with her tube feet. She humps her body over the cluster, clinging to the rock with just the tips of her arms. She stays humped this way for about forty days, until the young ones have hatched and can hold on with their own tube feet. She then flattens out but still stays with the brood for another twenty days. When she finally leaves them, each is about the size of a pinhead.

It's easy to get so absorbed by the tidepool that you forget to pay attention to where you are. This is a bad idea, because if you're on a raised spot, the incoming tide can cut you off from the beach before it gets your shoes wet. Set the alarm on your watch or carry a travel alarm in your pocket so that you'll know when visiting hours are ending.

I heard the water heaving up, filtering, settling, and coming again. Plants and animals clicked and gurgled. The open house was closing. I allowed myself to be ushered out, but would come back at high tide to see how far under the water I had been.

Back up on the beach, I wondered about all the little crab bodies strewn about. Pollution? Predators in the deep? Neither. They're not dead bodies at all, but merely the empty shells left behind after a natural molt. The crabs may still be out there somewhere, one size bigger.

Crabs, like most of their crustacean cousins, molt their shells periodically to allow for new growth. To tell the molted from the dead, pick up the next crab body you find and see if the carapace (the crab's back) lifts up like a jewelry box lid. The hinge is at the forehead because the crab backs out. Ever since I learned this bit of natural-history trivia I can't pass a crab shell without trying the lid. One of these times a ballerina is going to pop out.

When barnacles molt, they shed an outer skeleton, not a shell. This skeleton is outside the body but inside the protective plate that we scratch our elbows on. It's like they peel off their long underwear but leave their coveralls on.

If you can't make it for summer solstice, there are other tide-pooling opportunities. Monthly low tides occur within a few days of the new moon and the full moon. If you don't have a tide book, get one. They're cheap and often contain information on currents, sunrise, sunset, moonrise, and moonset as well as on tides. Notes in front explain how to read the tables; take care to read the right page (Pacific beach tides as opposed to Seattle tides, for example). Any −1.0 tide or lower is worth a special trip to the beach.

Mucking about in tidepools is a pleasure that carries certain responsibilities. We are guests, after all. Remember to put things back where you found them. Don't detach algae or animals such as barnacles or mussels that are fixed to the rocks because they will never reattach. If you turn over a rock to see what's underneath, take care not to crush what's living next door, and when you've had a look, replace the rock gently, right side up. Seaweeds help protect tidepool animals from drying out or getting too much sun; so if you pull aside plant coverings, tuck them back in before you move on. If you dig holes, refill them. Piled-up sand may suffocate clams and other burrowing animals underneath. Put clams just below the surface of the sand after you've filled a hole, not at the very bottom, where they might become trapped and suffocate. Think about how the plants and animals live in their community and who is dependent upon whom for food, shelter, or simply a place to attach.

Forgo taking souvenirs. Look at it as if you're rolling over your investment instead of making a withdrawal. Besides, whatever you take will probably stink by the time you get it home. At Rosario, as well as at many other public-access beaches, so many "grazers" (such as chitons, limpets, and snails) have been picked off by tidepool tourists that algae growth is going unchecked. As a result, rocky areas that once hosted a healthy balance of plants and animals are now slippery with overgrown algae and contain less diversity of species.

It's in our own interest to keep things healthy because we're

certain to be back—if not to this place, then to another, similar
one. Humans are drawn to the beach, some finding equilibrium
by the sea and others coming here to toe the edge. At Rosario it's
easy to feel the pull of the sea, to want to escort the tides out and
out to the margins of our own home zone.

Long ago in a different time, Ko-kwal-alwoot felt such a pull:

*A beautiful Samish girl, Ko-kwal-alwoot, was gathering
shellfish near Deception Pass when the clam she held slipped
from her hand. She kept retrieving and losing the clam,
following it farther and farther until she was waist deep in
the sea. When she bent to pick it up yet another time, a hand
met hers. A voice told her, "Don't be afraid, I only want to
admire your beauty."*

*The hand let go and Ko-kwal-alwoot went home. Each
time she went down to the water the hand took hers. The voice
said loving things to her and described a beautiful world at
the bottom of the sea. Finally one day, a young man rose up.
They went to the girl's father to ask permission to marry.*

*The father refused, afraid Ko-kwal-alwoot would drown.
The young man warned the father that he would take away
all the food they gathered from the sea, but the father would
not be moved.*

*Sure enough, in a short time, food became so scarce that
at last the father relented. He did ask that his daughter be
allowed to visit her people at least once a year, so they could
see she was all right.*

*Ko-kwal-alwoot waded into the outgoing tide to join her
husband as the people watched. The last thing they saw was
her long hair streaming in the current.*

*Once again, the sea became abundant. Ko-kwal-alwoot
returned every year for four years, but each time the people
noticed a change in the girl. Barnacles had begun to grow on
her hands and face, and on the fourth visit, she seemed
unhappy to be out of the water. A chill wind accompanied
her visits to the village.*

*The people felt sorry for her and released Ko-kwal-
alwoot's husband from his promise. Although she never
returned, the girl became a guardian of her people and they*

always had plenty of food from the sea. They knew she was watching over them, because they could see her long hair floating in the water.

—Adapted from Samish legend

A totem carving of the Maiden of Deception Pass stands over the tidepools of Rosario Beach. One side depicts the maiden before she took to the sea. On the other side, Ko-kwal-alwoot is bejeweled with fish and barnacles.

Maybe it was around the solstice that Ko-kwal-alwoot made her annual long walk back to land. Maybe on the solstice you could meet her halfway.

Timing Your Visit: The lowest tides of summer are always near the solstice, which is June 20 or 21. Check a tide book for specific dates and times.

Contact: For more information on Rosario Beach and Deception Pass State Park, contact Deception Pass State Park, 5175 N. State Highway 20, Oak Harbor, WA 98277; (206)675-2417.

Getting There: To get to Rosario Beach from Seattle, drive north on I-5 about 68 miles to the Highway 20 exit just north of Mount Vernon. Take Highway 20 west toward Anacortes. Before Anacortes, follow the main route of Highway 20 south. The beach turnoff is north of Deception Pass Bridge on the west side of the road.

Taking the Mukilteo ferry and driving up Whidbey Island is an alternate route.

Accommodations: For information on area facilities, contact the Anacortes Chamber of Commerce, 1319 Commercial, Anacortes, WA 98221; (206)293-3832.

WHERE ELSE TO GO TIDEPOOLING

WASHINGTON
Edmonds Beach, central Puget Sound, Washington: A beach ranger station and interpretive displays are part of this urban beach park

about 10 miles north of Seattle on Puget Sound. As a designated underwater park, Edmonds Beach is popular with scuba divers.

To get to Edmonds Beach from Seattle, take I-5 north and follow signs to the Edmonds–Kingston Ferry. Park just north of the ferry dock.

For more information on Edmonds Beach, contact the beach ranger station at 300 Admiral Way, Edmonds, WA 98020; (206)775-2525, ext. 271. For information on Edmonds area facilities, contact Edmonds Visitor Information, P.O. Box 146, Edmonds, WA 98020; (206)776-6711.

Seattle Aquarium, Seattle, Washington: Even if you can manage to catch the tides, a visit to a good aquarium is worthwhile. The Seattle Aquarium has an excellent marine invertebrate display, a touch tank, and offers special tours, classes, field trips, and lectures. The domed undersea viewing area can be an exciting place when stingrays and sharks weave by.

The Seattle Aquarium is located on Seattle's waterfront at Pier 59 near the downtown ferry terminal.

For more information, contact the Seattle Aquarium, 1483 Alaskan Way, Seattle, WA 98101; (206)386-4320. For information on Seattle area facilities, contact the Seattle/King County Convention and Visitors' Bureau, 520 Pike Street, Suite 1300, Seattle, WA 98101; (206)461-5840.

OREGON

Cape Perpetua Scenic Area, south-central coast, Oregon: Cape Perpetua offers tidepools for exploration and interpretive displays and computerized tide tables for enlightenment.

To get to Cape Perpetua from Newport, drive south on U.S. Highway 101. The cape is 3 miles south of Yachats.

For more information on Cape Perpetua Scenic Area, contact the Visitors' Center, P.O. Box 274, Yachats, OR 97498; (503)757-4480. For information on area facilities, contact the Yachats Area Chamber of Commerce, P.O. Box 174, Yachats, OR 97498; (503)547-3530.

Oregon Coast Aquarium, Newport, Oregon: Collectors for this new facility left no stone unturned in gathering Pacific Northwest anemones, sea stars, sea cucumbers, spiny urchins, and nudibranches for the rocky shore display. A touch pool is also entertaining.

The aquarium is located on the southern outskirts of Newport, off Ferry Slip Road.

For more information, contact the Oregon Coast Aquarium, P.O. Box 2000, Newport, OR 97365; (503)867-3474. For information on Newport area facilities, contact the Greater Newport Chamber of Commerce, 555 S.W. Coast Highway, Newport, OR 97365; (800)262-7844.

FALL

CHAPTER 11

WILD REVEILLE

Bugling Elk in Olympic National Park,
Washington

F rom a shadowed place inside the mossy sanctuary of ancient
forest, a piercing sound divides the silence. I can hear it mass
low in the belly of a big, warm-blooded body before it strains high
across a windpipe-reed into a surreal scream. The note holds clear
and then crashes down into tense, rhythmic grunts: *a-a-AH-AI-*
EEEEEEEEEEEEeeeee-eough! e-UNH! e-UNH! e-UNH!

Bull elk are bugling in the Hoh Rain Forest. This siren of
sexual desire will find a secret door in the back of your head and
corkscrew down your spine. If a cave painting could make a

sound, it would be this one.

In Olympic National Park's Hoh Rain Forest, huge old trees lean their heads together a hundred feet above a forest floor littered with immense fallen logs, berry bushes, ferns, and oxalis. The air is musky with decaying leaves and bark. And bugling.

The term *bugling* is a bit misleading—these bulls aren't blowing boogie-woogie. But, as with a bugle, a large volume of air is forced through a pipe to make a squeal. Folk wisdom has it that an elk uses its two prominent upper canine teeth—dubbed whistlers, ivories, or tusks—to make the sound. But in reality, the bull calls through his trachea, with antlers leveraged over his back, upper lip tight, tongue forward, and mouth cupped. *a-a-AH-EEEEEEEeeeee-unh!*

Boiled down to basics, bulls bugle from one motivation. Sex. They bugle to attract cows, to warn away other males, to trumpet their conquests, and simply because the spirit moves them. They begin to call early in the reproductive season when still in bachelor groups (talking it up with the boys?) and have been observed bugling to themselves as they wallow in mud and urine during the peak of the rut. The breeding season, or rut, for elk on the western side of the Cascade Mountains typically begins in early September and peaks in mid- to late September or early October. East of the mountains, bulls come on a little later. Cows don't bugle, although they do have a repertoire of grunts, barks, and squeaks.

Outside the breeding season, elk tend to be matriarchal, living in groups of cows, calves, and subadults of both sexes, guided by an elder female. Herds can consist of five or six to fifty or more animals, depending upon the circumstances. Breeding-age bulls gather in their own groups and usually stay hidden in heavy cover until they move out to assemble harems in the fall. A bull may collect anywhere from a few to a dozen or more cows, depending on his virility and his vigilance in keeping his concubines together and away from other males. If a bull takes over an entire cow herd, subadult males are driven off for the time being, but often rejoin the females after the rut.

A young bull begins to test his voice when he's about two years old; cows generally show no interest in the cracking, adolescent overtures. By age three the bull has found his voice but is usually not competitive enough to claim a harem. After one or two such frustrating seasons, his physical and vocal stature finally match his desire and he wins or woos his first cows.

As the young bull's voice grows and matures, so do his antlers. The first year they're ten- to twelve-inch spikes set high on the bone stem. Each spring he sheds them and grows a new set. Antlers, such as those grown by male elk, deer, and moose, are shed every year. In most antlered animals, only the male grows the headpiece. Caribou are the exception to this rule—both male and female caribou grow antlers.

Horns, such as those found on bighorn sheep and mountain goats, are grown by both male and female, although the male's are typically much larger. Unlike antlers, true horns are never shed.

Even though the antlers of a two-year-old bull elk may branch into four or five tines, or points, the rack of a young male is still relatively small and light. A three year old may have the same number of points, but his antlers will be sturdier and the bone stems shorter and thicker. By age four, he could break into the six-point ranks. A "six-point" bull has six tines on each antler and is considered well-developed.

Although antler development is linked to age, you can't definitively age a bull by the number of points he carries on his head. Nutrition and physical condition are the ultimate controlling factors in antler size. An old bull past his prime may regress to spikes, and the racks of malnourished bulls may be stunted.

Big racks are luxury items. Energy goes into antler growth only after all other nutritional needs are met; so large antlers advertise strength and a successful lifestyle. Bulls flash big racks the way some men flash American Express Gold Cards. Cows get the message and allow themselves to be selected by the bulls with Calvin Klein genes.

Getting down to business, antlers can be savage weapons, but more often they are reserved for creating effect. Agitated bulls turn tree saplings into stropping leathers, stripping the bark and staining their racks reddish brown in the process. By the end of the rut, these small trees may look like they've been hit by heat lightning. Which, in a way, they have been.

When an outsider bull bugles a challenge, the herd bull

bellows back, steps out where the interloper can see him, and proceeds to rake the undergrowth into curried patches. The bits of shrubbery and divots of moss that become entangled in his antlers turn the rack into a warrior chief's headdress, which he wears with pride.

As he rakes, he pees. In fact, creative urination is a big part of bullhood. A bull can turn the nozzle of urination from spray to stream and direct the flow according to his whim. He soaks his belly hair and then lowers his head and sprays his mane and face. The urine stains his coat dark and, together with the huckleberry headdress, creates a larger-than-life visual and olfactory image for cows and potential challengers.

Even after the challenger is gone, the bull may shower the ground beneath him and roll in it. Wallowing seems to take place only during the rut. Bulls dig and mix wallows in wet meadows and spend hours rolling in this pheromonal mud bath while cows gambol giddily or coyly nearby.

Some bulls become so consumed with the whole rutting scene that they stop eating. A bull that goes into the season looking like the king of the forest may come out resembling a walking road-kill. Surplus fat has been used up, and he may enter winter in a weakened state. Cougars and sometimes bears will cull the weakest animals, benefiting both predator and prey. Cows, on the other hand, have been free during the rut to fatten up and are better prepared to meet cold weather and support the fetuses growing inside them.

The Shawnees called elk *wapiti,* meaning "white rump," a reference to the light-colored rump patch that makes elk easier to spot on a hillside. Wapiti, which once ranged across most of North America, were gone from the eastern states by about 1850, from the plains states by 1870, and from much of the Southwest by the late 1800s. Market hunters, farmers, and ranchers cleared out whole populations. Around the end of the nineteenth century, added pressure came from the ironically named Benevolent Protective Order of Elks. Wapiti "ivories" became the central icon for club members, and this demand for tooth watch fobs, rings, and other trinkets pushed already shrunken populations over the edge. At President

elk ivory

Theodore Roosevelt's request, the B.P.O.E. membership finally renounced the use of elk tooth adornments and went on to work for elk preservation. Still, from an estimated 10 million in 1760, the nation's elk population had dwindled to 70,000 by 1919. Two subspecies became extinct during that time: the Merriam elk of the Southwest and the eastern elk of the Great Lakes region and southern United States.

Four North American elk subspecies survive today: the Roosevelt elk, Manitoba elk, Rocky Mountain elk, and California's Tule elk, the latter coming to within one breeding pair of extinction. Only Roosevelt and Rocky Mountain elk are found in Washington and Oregon.

Originally, Rocky Mountain elk were found from the Rocky Mountains west to eastern Washington and Oregon. They were eliminated from much of their range by market hunters and settlers, but the ruggedness and inaccessibility of the Rockies saved those herds from total annihilation. In more recent history, elk from the Rocky Mountains have been used to reintroduce herds to many western states, including Washington and Oregon, and have also been successfully transplanted outside their historical range.

Roosevelt elk could once be found all along the western side of the Cascade Mountains from Canada down into California, but most of their range has been staked out by humans, who also seem to like living on the coast. Remaining Roosevelt elk populations in northern California, Western Oregon, Western Washington, and Vancouver Island, Canada, are now isolated from one another.

Although Rocky Mountain elk are more abundant and generally easier to observe than Roosevelts, sharing ghost-space in a misty old-growth forest with the larger bodied, darker Roosevelt elk approaches a mystical experience. About 5,000 Roosevelt elk filter through Olympic National Park river valleys and forests, and twice that many roam the Olympic Peninsula outside park boundaries. Protection of the Roosevelt elk was a major impetus for creating the park in 1938.

One herd claims the Hoh Rain Forest campground in Olympic National Park as part of its home range. In late fall and winter, elk occasionally wander right past the picnic tables, although more often they are spotted on the nature trails leading out from the visitor center. Elk are most active, and most likely to bugle, at dawn and dusk.

Besides the nature trails, the road paralleling the Hoh River is a good place to look and listen. Tracks and wet spots or droppings along the road are signs to pull over and check out the river or woods. Sometimes you have to go by intuition—or by the fact that another car has pulled over, which is as important a sign to watch for as droppings. Park the car and scramble through the underbrush to a high bank overlooking the wide gravel bars of the Hoh. Listen, sniff the wind, even bugle yourself if the night is too quiet.

One lucky twilight, a little knot of friends and I hadn't been standing over the river's edge for two minutes when a bugle floated through the air from across the river. A call answered from somewhere below.

Two bulls squared off on opposite sides of the river as we strained to see in the failing light. Across the Hoh, a large bull levitated from out of the dense cover. He gathered his air and pushed it into a high, full-bellied scream, which he sustained and then let crash down into tense grunts. On our side of the water, we heard heavy hooves scrape aside rocks, and the second bull lifted his head into view. He swung his rack slow as a heavy sigh and answered in a thin wail. The exchange must have carried a clear message for each elk since neither bugled again.

We returned early the next morning to wander the riverbank and look for signs of the previous night's phantoms. Pausing in a stand of white-barked, lichen-flocked alder, we listened to the trees whisper secrets to each other over our heads, but they offered no clues. The sand and mud were a bit more forthcoming, displaying to us animal tracks laid down like lines of type: birds skittering one way, maybe a mink crossing the trail, raccoon paws pausing at a quiet eddy under the willows. Elk scat confirmed we were on the right track, but we never caught up.

I tried to conjure the elusive wapiti with my plastic elk bugle and cow call, but with no luck and only minor embarrassment. Hunters use these gizmos to locate bulls and draw them in close. The bugle is a twenty-five-inch-long, flexible plastic tube covered in camouflage cloth. Two-thirds of the mouthpiece is covered by a taut piece of latex rubber. The idea is to curl down your lower lip, press it against the latex, and blow across the edge. "Blow from your stomach," advise the experts. Bugling takes a lot of air.

elk hunter's bugle

Cow calls are easier and work well early in the rut for bringing out bulls. The cow call is a flat piece of plastic half the size of a playing card that makes the same kind of sound you get from blowing on a piece of grass held tight between your thumbs. The guy at the sporting goods store who showed me how to use each one said I made a better cow. He said this with a straight face.

You don't have to sound exactly like an elk to get a response; maybe they're just letting you know that they know. Or maybe they're laughing at you, or irritated you would even try such a fool thing.

My friends and I gave up on the riverbank and headed back toward the road. Even though the elk weren't visible, their presence was evident in the suite of surrounding forest. Roosevelt elk play an important role in the evolution of an old-growth forest. They keep the understory open by browsing on trees, berry bushes, grasses, ferns, and fungi. This clearance promotes new growth and helps shape plant diversity. Herds spend a few days grazing in one spot and move on to another area of their home range, not returning for several weeks.

By the time we reached the truck it was day, not morning, and the chances of seeing elk before evening had reached lottery odds. But it had been a rich outing nonetheless, decorated by storytelling tracks, heart-shaped rocks, feathers, antler-rubbed trees, and the spirit-lifting warble of winter wrens.

The thick forest conceals its residents. But rivers, meadows, and trails are like hotel hallways where elk slip out of one room and into another right before the elevator doors open. You won't see much if you keep riding the elevator up and down, but if you sit in the hall for a while, you might get an eyeful.

It's a bit of a trek over to the Hoh, but the musky allure of lusty ungulates in the rain forest is strongly compelling. Share the drive with someone you love.

Timing Your Visit: West of the Cascade Range, the rut typically peaks in mid- to late September. East of the Cascades, the rut is slightly later, peaking in early- to mid-October.

Contact: For more information on Olympic National Park and the Hoh Rain Forest, contact the Park Superintendent, Olympic National Park, 600 E. Park Avenue, Port Angeles, WA 98362; (206)452-4501.

Getting There: To get to the Hoh Rain Forest from Port Angeles, take U.S. Highway 101 west about 72 miles through Forks to the Upper Hoh Road. The Hoh Campground and Rain Forest Visitors' Center are at the end of the Upper Hoh Road, about 19 miles in.

Accommodations: For information on Olympic Peninsula facilities, contact the Olympic Peninsula Tourism Council, 120 Washington Avenue, Suite 101-A, Bremerton, WA 98310; (206)479-3599.

WHERE ELSE TO SEE BUGLING ELK

Note: No hunting is permitted in national parks, but hunting may be allowed in wildlife areas and national forests. Hunting seasons may occasionally coincide with the rut, so check with the state wildlife department to find out when the seasons are so you can avoid those areas.

WASHINGTON
Oak Creek Wildlife Area, south-central Washington: Rocky Mountain elk bugle in this area from late September through mid-October.

To get to Oak Creek Wildlife Area from Yakima, take Highway 12 west through Naches, past the junction with Highway 410. The wildlife area visitor center is located about 2 miles past the junction.

For more information on Oak Creek Wildlife Area, contact the Washington Department of Wildlife, 2802 Fruitvale Boulevard, Yakima, WA 98902; (509)575-2740. For information on area facilities, contact the South Central Washington Tourism

Council, P.O. Box 1490, Yakima, WA 98907; (509)248-2021.

John's River Wildlife Area, southwestern Washington: You can hear Roosevelt elk bugling in this area from about mid- to late September.

To get to John's River Wildlife Area from Aberdeen, take Highway 105 along the south shore of Grays Harbor. A footpath runs along the dike on the south side of John's River, and other trails are accessible off Highway 105 and John's River Road. Another section of the wildlife area lies a few miles northwest of Raymond and can be reached on back roads from Highway 105 or Highway 101.

For more information on John's River Wildlife Area, contact the Washington Department of Wildlife, 905 E. Heron, Aberdeen, WA 98520; (206)533-9335. For information on area facilities, contact the Grays Harbor Tourism Council, 2109 Sumner Avenue, Suite 202, Aberdeen, WA 98520; (206)456-0158.

OREGON

Dean Creek Elk-viewing Area, south-central Oregon: Roosevelt elk are easily seen at this viewing area. Bugling is at its peak in mid-September to early October.

To get to the Dean Creek Elk-viewing Area from Eugene, take Highway 126 to Florence. At Florence, take Highway 101 south to Reedsport. The viewing area is 3 miles east of Reedsport on Highway 38.

For more information on Dean Creek Elk-viewing Area, contact the Bureau of Land Management, Coos Bay District, 333 S. Fourth Street, Coos Bay, OR 97420; (503)269-5880. For information on area facilities, contact the Lower Umpqua Chamber of Commerce, Box 11-B, Reedsport, OR 97467; (800)247-2155; or outside Oregon, (503)271-3495.

Jewell Meadows Wildlife Area, northern coast of Oregon: Jewell Meadows, located about 60 miles northwest of Portland, is an important wintering area for Roosevelt elk. Bugling extends from mid-September to mid-October. Elk are also sometimes seen from the Sunset Highway Forest Wayside Nature Trail, back down

Highway 26 toward Portland.

To get to Jewell Meadows from Portland, take Highway 26 to Jewell Junction and then take an unmarked road 9 miles north to Jewell. The meadows are a little over a mile west of Jewell on Highway 202.

For more information on Jewell Meadows Wildlife Area, contact the Oregon Department of Fish and Wildlife, P.O. Box 59, Portland, OR 97207; (503)229-5403. For information on area facilities, contact the Northwest Oregon Visitors' Center, 25 S.W. Salmon, Portland, OR 97240; (503)222-2223.

CHAPTER 12

CARRY ME BACK TO WILLIAM FINLEY

Canada Geese at William L. Finley National Wildlife Refuge, Oregon

The time I wish most desperately to fly is in the fall, when Canada geese pass *uh-honking* overhead, steaming south. It's agony to be left behind.

But I have heard of stories, told by Native Americans and goose hunters, about geese taking passengers during the migration. The stories probably aren't true, and even if they were, I still couldn't join the cackling choir, because the passengers are other birds. Little birds—sparrows and finches, according to the Cree Indians who lived along Hudson Bay and the Crow Indians of Montana, and hummingbirds, according to certain hunters who claim to have found hummingbirds tucked into the feathers of downed geese. One hunter carried a live hummingbird in a tobacco pouch to show his friend, so the story goes.

Passengers or no, millions of geese, ducks, and swans migrate through Washington and Oregon every year on the way south from their summer ranges in Canada and Alaska. Along the route are a few strategically located refuges that serve as waystops for migrating waterfowl. At William L. Finley National Wildlife Refuge, near Corvallis in the Willamette Valley of western Oregon, grasses and grains are grown especially to feed the waterfowl; marshes provide safe places to rest. For thousands of migrants, Finley Refuge is also an end-of-the-line winter destination.

The 5,325-acre reserve drapes over gentle hills in a patchwork of woodlands, farm fields, marshes, meadows, and pastures, cross-stitched by hedgerows of maple and Oregon white oak. Trees, old fence posts, and just about everything that doesn't move or get mowed is swaddled in soft moss and hung by old man's beard lichen. On a foggy morning, the shaggy landscape is straight from a fairy tale where witches have warts and trees point gnarly fingers at lost children. But when the sun burns through, instead of children you see geese and ducks, and they know exactly where they are and why they are there.

Migrating waterfowl begin showing up in the Willamette Valley in mid-October. By mid-November, large numbers of Canada geese, tundra swans, and a variety of ducks, including pintails, mallards, green-winged teal, American wigeon, and northern shovelers, are brightening Finley Refuge fields and ponds. In the air, wobbly shoestrings of dark geese and white swans lace the surrounding hills to the low sky.

Since, technically, I can't join the migration, I do the next best thing: drive as long as it takes to feel far from home and then keep going until I hear gravel scrunching under the tires. The gravel on Finley Refuge roads is satisfyingly scrunchy, and roadside snowberries and rosehips add to the feeling of fall. .

Migration is wildlife's way of pacing off the seasons. By the time snow and cold are poised over northern breeding grounds, downy babies have grown into firm-feathered adolescents. On cue, birds blow south like autumn leaves. Although many species of birds—from warblers to pelicans—fly south for the winter, the sight of migrating geese feels most synonymous with fall.

The term *waterfowl* refers to ducks, geese, and swans. Other families of birds are associated with water but are called something else. Sandpipers and dunlins, for instance, are lumped into a large group known as shorebirds; great blue herons and egrets are wading birds. Puffins and murres are two of many seabirds, and pelicans belong to a miscellaneous group called water birds. Gulls will be gulls.

For all their differences, many species of seabirds, shorebirds, water birds, and waterfowl have one thing in common: migration. We know the who, where, and when of migration, and we know basically why. But the how remains one of life's sweeter mysteries.

Most migration is along a north-south line, but birds may also migrate diagonally, or from one altitude to another within the same few square miles. The motivation—the why—is survival. Popular avian breeding grounds in Alaska and Canada may meet the food and space requirements of nesting, but these places freeze over in the winter. And while wintering areas may have open water and food, there are probably not enough overall resources to support year-round residents. Of course, not all birds or animals migrate, but if none did, huge expanses of habitat would go unused while others would be destroyed by overuse. Migration helps keep the ecological teeter-totter in balance.

Four north-south migratory flyways—the Pacific, Central, Mississippi, and Atlantic—roll over North American air space like invisible superhighways. Although some species, such as mallards and Canada geese, occur in all four, each flyway contains a distinct set of species and subspecies.

Southbound Pacific Flyway waterfowl begin arriving in the Northwest in early October. They travel day and night, following specific migration corridors within the general flyway. Renowned waterfowl researcher Frank Bellrose, who originated the idea of corridors within flyways, describes the subdivisions as thirty- to fifty-mile-wide routes that follow river valleys or chains of lakes or marshes.

Geese, much more family-oriented than ducks, travel the fly-ways in flocks composed of banded-together family units. It is generally thought that flocks of Canada geese, which can range in size from a few to a few hundred, are led by a dominant gander. (The male is a "gander," the female a "goose." And if you want to sound like you know what you're talking about, always say "Canada" geese, never "Canadian" geese.) Jet pilots have reported Canada geese flying at 20,000 feet, although cruising altitudes of 1,000 to 3,000 feet are more common. Flight speed ranges from forty to sixty miles per hour. For years, their V formation was explained in terms of flight efficiency. It seems reasonable, and when theories of lift are applied to the question, mathematics proves that flying in perfect formation, with each bird one-quarter wingspan behind the one ahead, allows birds to fly 71 percent farther for the same amount of energy. But actual film footage reveals that geese don't continually hold to such precise formation. So now scientists are thinking that geese fly in Vs to keep each other in sight and avoid collisions. Everyone agrees on one thing: "Further study is required."

Whether they fly in Vs, Us, lines, or flocks, migrating birds probably get where they're going by a combination of methods. Bellrose has seen migrating geese change direction by thirty-five to forty degrees over certain landmarks. Geese, ducks, and other birds are also thought to reckon by the sun and stars and possibly use cues from the earth's magnetic field.

It wouldn't matter how they found their way if they couldn't survive the trip. Migrating waterfowl need places to rest and eat along the way—places like the William L. Finley Refuge. To prove it, they show up in droves.

Tundra swans are Finley's visiting celebrities, and the assorted ducks with their blue bills, green heads, and orange feet add color. But Canada geese are indisputably the dominant presence here. This is fitting, considering the refuge was established especially to provide protection for dusky geese, a subspecies of Canada goose.

Seven of the eleven subspecies of Canada goose occur in the Northwest. In order of size from largest to smallest, they are the western (or Great Basin), Vancouver, dusky, Taverner's, lesser, Aleutian, and cackling. They all look basically alike, with the typical Canada goose gray-brown body, black head and neck, and white chinstrap. The subspecies, which commonly mingle in mixed flocks, are classified according to size, head shape, color, body proportion, voice, call pattern, and home range.

Sizes range from the ten-pound western Canada goose to the mallard-size cackler. Among the three or four biggest subspecies, size and color differences can be subtle. The western has a light breast, which helps distinguish it from the slightly smaller Vancouver, which has a dark breast.

The dusky, one size down from the Vancouver, is a distinctive chocolate brown, with a neck that seems to merge with its darkish breast. The slightly smaller Taverner's has a lighter breast and is more likely than a dusky to have a faint, light-colored ring around the base of its neck.

Before 1970, the goose flock at Finley Refuge was almost exclusively duskys. Cacklers are now the most common winter goose there, followed by Taverner's and then lessers. Vancouvers and westerns are also present.

In sorting them all out, knowing their respective sizes and subtleties of plumage is great, but plastic neck collars are the definitive clue. Only a small portion of Pacific Flyway geese are col-lared, but if you spot one, you can compare it to the others. Duskys wear red collars, cacklers yellow, and westerns gray. Taverner's have not been collared as of yet.

neck collar

Like the extended family they are, Canada geese all share a name and certain physical features. But also like most extended families, some branches are doing better than others. Westerns are sitting at the head table these days. This subspecies is expanding both its numbers and its range. The Aleutian cousins haven't been riding quite as high, but at least they're still coming to the party. Numbers are increasing, and the Aleutian Canada goose was offi-cially downlisted from endangered to threatened in 1991. Availability of winter range, conditions on breeding grounds, and hunting pressure are the three most important factors influencing which subspecies prosper and which don't. Duskys have suffered setbacks in all three.

The entire dusky population winters in small areas of the Willamette Valley and lower Columbia River. Creation in the mid-1960s of the Finley Refuge and two other refuges in the Willamette Valley—Baskett Slough and Ankeny—helped offset the loss of wintering habitat to agriculture and urban sprawl. But just as the problem of winter range was being addressed, big problems were shaking out on the breeding grounds. When an earthquake measuring 8.5 on the Richter scale slammed the Alaskan landscape in 1964, the earthquake zone included the Copper River Delta near Cordova, where duskys have been breeding since people began remembering such things.

The earthquake lifted parts of the delta two to six feet. As a result, the ecosystem slowly began to change. Before the quake, sedge grasses were the dominant vegetation. Sedge meadows, cut by sloughs, are ideal for nesting. Visibility is good, there is plenty of grass to eat, and the sloughs act as moats to protect eggs and goslings from mammalian predators. But, after the earthquake, willows and alders grew on the uplifted land and encroached on the remaining marsh, where geese continued to nest. Bears and coyotes moved into the new brushy habitat and found the geese easy prey. Studies in the 1980s found that two-thirds of dusky nests were being destroyed and an unusually high number of adult geese were being killed.

Like most subspecies of Canada goose, duskys are extremely faithful to their traditional nesting areas. The female picks a nest site the first year she lays, and then she and her lifelong mate return to the same spot year after year. So even though the quality and quantity of Copper River Delta nesting habitat was reduced, the duskys keep going back.

Off the breeding grounds, human hunters also took a toll on the dusky, which is one of the least wary of Canada geese. When the population hit its all-time low of 7,500 birds in 1984, wildlife officials enacted regulations designed to severely limit the harvest of duskys. In the initial regulations, a hunter who shot a dusky was not ticketed but lost all hunting privileges for the rest of that season and the next. Required hunter-education identification programs and self-policing by hunters helped reduce the number of duskys killed, and the regulations were relaxed. Currently, if a hunter shoots a dusky, only the remainder of that season is forfeited.

Fewer hunting mortalities, the construction of more than 500 artificial nesting islands on the Copper River Delta, and continued protection of wintering grounds such as the Finley Refuge are all contributing to dusky recovery. Numbers are currently estimated to be holding steady at about 12,000, but the long-term prognosis is unclear.

Weighing down the other end of the teeter-totter is the western Canada goose. It's true what they say about success breeding contempt. Complaints against westerns are on the rise. The big geese are in competition with golf-course gardeners who complain of overgrazed greens, with picnickers and park-goers who complain there's not a clean, blanket-sized square of ground to sit on, and with officials who worry that goose droppings might foul city water supplies. Westerns nest in patio planter boxes, docked ski boats, and on the decks of waterfront condominiums.

The presence of wildlife in an urban setting raises new issues and forces us to face our relationship with animals and nature. We identify urban wildlife as a good thing but complain when a goose gets obnoxious or a raccoon won't leave the porch. I like visiting refuges because spending time in a place where other species have the right-of-way helps me keep things in perspective.

Near the pullout by McFadden's Marsh at the southeast corner of the refuge, 2,000 geese forgot I was there about two seconds after I turned off the engine. Geese feeding and children in a schoolyard sound a lot alike. I studied the mass of geese rip, rip, ripping up grass just beyond the car and tried to pick out the duskys.

Watching a flock of geese is like sitting in the dark and letting your eyes adjust. The longer you look, the more you see. You start to pick out families and pairs and begin to notice squabbles, negotiations, and good-to-see-ya greetings.

Among the milling crowd, one goose stopped grazing. It straightened up and began to yap. Five birds around it oriented themselves in the same general direction. The protagonist gave its head a series of shakes, yapped again, took four steps, and suddenly a family of six whirred up together, wresting themselves from the larger flock to move to another field. A different family, on its way in, spied the opening and circled over the spot. Shoulders forward, necks stretched out to watch the ground between their splayed black feet, they turned into the wind and fluttered to earth.

A goose family stays together until the next breeding season, when the adults are ready to bring on the next generation. The newly independent juveniles will find mates by their third year. Stories about Canada goose attacks usually involve some unfortunate soul who gets between a goose or gander and its family. Pairs are steadfastly loyal to each other. If one in a pair is injured and unable to fly, its mate will stay behind and try to protect it. If one is lost, the other invests time and energy in a frantic, honking search for its mate.

Either is a very distressing spectacle to witness, made even more disheartening by the fact that there is nothing you can say to a goose to convey your sympathy. Just like there is no way in this world I will ever hitch passage on a migrating goose and ride it through a cold night in a sky full of diamonds. But I can send my heart high with the honking hosannas and head for the hills.

Timing Your Visit: Migrating waterfowl begin to arrive at William L. Finley National Wildlife Refuge in October. Numbers reach their peak in mid-November.

Contact: For more information, contact William L. Finley Refuge headquarters, 26208 Finley Refuge Road, Corvallis, OR 97333; (503)757-7236.

Getting There: The William L. Finley Refuge is about 12 miles south of Corvallis off Highway 99W. The clearly marked entrance is on the west side of the road. Refuge headquarters, housed in a renovated, 1912 hunting lodge, is off Finley Refuge Road across from the big, red barn.

Accommodations: For information on Corvallis area facilities, contact the Corvallis Visitors' Bureau, 420 N.W. Second, Corvallis, OR 97330; (800)757-1544.

WHERE ELSE TO SEE MIGRATING WATERFOWL

WASHINGTON
Ridgefield National Wildlife Refuge, southwestern Washington:

Dusky geese use this Columbia River refuge north of Vancouver, Washington. Ridgefield contains farmland, marshes, ponds, and pastures—all big draws for migrating waterfowl. Besides the duskys, look for tundra swans, cinnamon teal, wigeon, mallards, pintails, shovelers, and gadwalls.

To get to Ridgefield National Wildlife Refuge from Vancouver, take I-5 north to the Ridgefield exit. Go west 3 miles to Ridgefield; refuge headquarters is at 210 N. Main Street.

For information on Ridgefield National Wildlife Refuge, contact refuge headquarters, 210 N. Main Street, Ridgefield, WA 98642; (206)887-4071. For information on area facilities, contact the Vancouver–Clark County Visitor Bureau, 404 E. 15th Street, Suite 11, Vancouver, WA 98663; (206)694-1313.

Turnbull National Wildlife Refuge, east-central Washington: During the fall migration as many as 50,000 waterfowl may use this refuge. A self-guided auto tour route passes several water impoundments. Western Canada geese are found here, as well as cinnamon teal, ruddy ducks, wood ducks, pintails, redheads, buffleheads, shovelers, wigeon, canvasbacks, and gadwalls.

To get to Turnbull National Wildlife Refuge from Spokane, take I-90 west and then Highway 904 to Cheney. Turn left on Cheney Plaza Road to the refuge entrance.

For more information on Turnbull National Wildlife Refuge, contact refuge headquarters, Route 3, Box 385, Cheney, WA 99004; (509)235-4723. For information on area facilities, contact the Cheney Chamber of Commerce, P.O. Box 65, Cheney, WA 99004; (509)235-8480.

OREGON
Sauvie Island Wildlife Area, northwestern Oregon: This 12,000-acre wildlife area near Portland hosts more than 300,000 ducks and geese during the peak of fall migration. Some areas are closed during hunting season, which runs from late October to late January.

To get to Sauvie Island from Portland, take Highway 30 toward St. Helens. In about 10 miles, turn right onto the Sauvie Island Bridge. Get the required parking permit at the wildlife area headquarters on Sauvie Island Road or at the store at the end of the Sauvie Island Bridge.

For more information on Sauvie Island Wildlife Area, contact the Oregon Department of Fish and Wildlife, P.O. Box 59, Portland, OR 97207; (503)621-3488. For information on Portland area facilities, contact the Portland/Oregon Visitors' Association, 26 S.W. Salmon, Portland, OR 97204; (503)222-2223, or, outside Oregon, (800)345-3214.

Ladd Marsh Wildlife Area, northeastern Oregon: Ladd Marsh is one of the few remaining bulrush marshes in northeastern Oregon. Access is limited, but viewpoints are scattered along the Foothill–Ladd Canyon Road. A nature trail cuts through one corner of the marsh.

To get to Ladd Marsh from La Grande, go south on I-84 for about 5 miles and then take exit 268 to the Foothill–Ladd Canyon Road.

For more information about Ladd Marsh Wildlife Area, contact the Oregon Department of Fish and Wildlife, Box 339, La Grande, OR 97850; (503)963-2138. For information on area facilities, contact the La Grande–Union County Chamber of Commerce, 1502 N. Pine, La Grande, OR, 97850; (503)963-8588.

CHAPTER 13

THEY DO RUN RUN

Pronghorns at Hart Mountain National Antelope Refuge, Oregon

When pronghorns run, they *run.* Like there is nothing else on earth worth doing. They gallop hard, heads held steady, ears tuned forward, faces set in tight little smiles of speed.

When settlers first crossed the Great Plains they mistook pronghorns for Old World antelope, much in the same way they mistook bison for buffalo. Pronghorns are not closely related to true antelope and are, in fact, among the most native of all North American hoofed mammals. Their ancestors were established on this continent millions of years ago when the other ungulates, including deer, elk, moose, and bison, were waiting for the Bering Land Bridge to form so they could walk over from Europe and Asia.

Many of those newcomer species adapted to a variety of habitats. The pronghorn, however, remained purely a creature of open space, keeping to sagebrush deserts and grassland prairies. After a million years in virtually the same form in the same habitat, the pronghorn has become as specialized and efficient as a desert flower. It has speed in a land of few obstructions and keen vision to inform its world clear to the horizon.

The largest group of pronghorns in the Pacific Northwest lives in a corner of Oregon that is more Nevada than Northwest. A place where you can drive all day down a dirt road and still be less than halfway to nowhere. A timeless place of fault-block mountains, greasewood, twisted juniper, horizon, silence, and stars. A place where, okay, the antelope play.

The 275,000-acre Hart Mountain National Antelope Refuge (traditionally named, if not exactly correct) is home to several hundred pronghorns. Carry water, binoculars, a good map, and a sense of adventure. October is a good time to see larger herds of animals as they are beginning to collect in wintering groups. Most refuge roads aren't paved and there's no feeding station or accommodating band of semidomestic creatures posing for Polaroids. But there's plenty to see, and a visitor-generated list of "notable wildlife observations" in the refuge's tiny self-service interpretive center gives you clues where to start looking:

"Saw twenty antelope by Spanish Lake, early morning. Lake is totally dry."

"Observed five bighorn sheep on the east slope of Poker Jim Ridge. One really big ram."

"Wild horses!! by Desert Lake."

"One lazuli bunting in the aspens at Hot Springs Campground."

"Fifty antelope and a few mule deer on the road to Black Canyon."

"One rattler. Since deceased."

The best bet for seeing pronghorns is on the dried lake beds scattered around the refuge. Even in years of normal precipitation, many of the lakes indicated on your map will be dried out by midsummer. When the water is gone, grassy forbs grow up through the dry ground like a kept promise. Pronghorns come to graze, sometimes in the hundreds. During the last few years of drought, however, the promise appears to have been reneged. Snowfall has been too light to feed all the lakes adequately, so many of the beds have become cracked and hard. Refuge managers have had to excavate small pools to make sure animals have access to water. I mistook the first little reservoir I saw for a bright blue tarp, so vivid was the reflected sky and so unexpected the water.

But the lake beds are still good places to start the search, and during my visit, the ranger had recommended Spanish Lake in the southeastern corner of the refuge.

Driving along the dirt roads, roiling up great plumes of autumn dust, I didn't worry about trying to sneak up on the pronghorns. It's impossible. Their eight-power eyesight detects movement three miles away. Fortunately, confidence in their own ability to see danger coming and get away fast keeps them from being unreasonably flighty. They seem to prefer to keep you in sight, running only far enough to feel out of reach.

Spanish Lake was covered with dried grass. From a distance, I saw what looked to be flowing, light brown lava. Looking harder through the curtain of heat waves, I saw churning legs kicking up a shimmering hedge of dust. Even in mid-October, the temperature was near eighty degrees.

The pronghorns stopped on a low rise a short distance away and looked back, their black horns and noses lined up like an audience waiting for a punch line. About the size of a small deer, the pronghorn has a unique color patterning. On a base coat of russet, a white belly patch comes nearly halfway up its sides, and white crescents drape across the front of its neck like a couple of cowboy bandannas. Its chest and rump are also white, as is the bottom of its face in a line from nose to eye.

Of all the land animals in the world, only the cheetah is faster. Pronghorns have a spurt speed of sixty miles per hour and can sustain speeds of thirty to forty for longer distances. The absence of dew claws gives the pronghorn the most streamlined foot of any of the 200 species of even-toed ungulate.

But, for pronghorns, the act of running transcends statistics and details of natural history. Accounts abound of them racing cars and horses in seemingly the same spirit that dolphins play in a boat's wake. Pioneers and early naturalists were struck by the animal's unyielding determination to run in a straight line no matter what wagon or pack train lay in its path. Not that pronghorns aren't agile—a favorite tactic involves suddenly veering in front of a gaining aggressor and ruining the momentum of the chase. It's just that the full-speed-ahead strategy worked fine through the millennia until humans changed the landscape status quo.

Fences caught them entirely off guard. Although pronghorns can long-jump fourteen feet on the run, they can't, or at least won't, leap over things. After a couple of centuries of trial and error, pronghorns have learned to squeeze under the arbitrary wire borders or slip between their strands. I've seen a panicked pronghorn try to jump a low, barbed-wire fence but tangle its leg on the way over and get thrown to the ground. Before I could sort out the images of me flinging a coat over its head and freeing it, and me with a broken nose and no teeth, the thrashing animal freed itself, still on the same side of the fence.

Animal predators provided the original incentive to run and dodge, but the most effective ones, including the wolf, grizzly, and cougar, are now almost entirely gone from the pronghorn's range. The remaining animal predators, largely coyotes, bobcats, and eagles, don't bother adults much but are known to take fawns. Predators must be tricky to succeed, however, as fawns find their legs early in life and adults see trouble coming a long way off. The pronghorn has huge eyes, which give it a tremendous scope of vision for detecting and evading predators. Thick eyelashes reduce glare. Given the fact that keen eyesight comprises much of the pronghorn's defense, its renowned curiosity makes sense. It *needs* to see everything there is to see.

Native Americans, and later white settlers, found they could lure pronghorns into killing range by hiding in the grass and waving a brightly colored flag. Pronghorns were such easy targets that, by the early 1900s, populations had dropped from about 40 million to about 13,000. Hunting was closed for twenty-five years and the species recovered to its present level of about 800,000. Nowadays, pronghorns are hunted throughout the West, including a limited season at Hart Mountain.

Pronghorns are the only species in their family, Antilocapridae.

One of the reasons they have their own family stems from the unique fact that they regularly shed their horns. North America's other horned mammals belong to the Bovidae family, whose members don't shed their horns. Sheep, goats, and bison are all bovids. A third family, the Cervidae (deer, elk, moose, and caribou), have antlers, which are shed every year.

Both male and female pronghorns have horns, although the female's rarely grow longer than a few inches. The male's grow to about a foot, with the tips sweeping back like plow handles past a blunt, thorn-shaped spike about midway up. The pronghorn is the only animal in the world with horns that branch.

Even though they are shed annually, pronghorns don't grow like antlers, which completely drop off and grow back essentially from scratch every year. Nor do they grow precisely like the more similarly composed bovid horns. Pronghorns start out as a bony core growing from the skull. Each year a furry "skin" grows over this core and hardens into a sheath of the same keratinous material that makes hooves and fingernails. As the bone core inside grows larger over time, the sheath eventually splits and falls off. The core is liberated to the air like a mended broken arm from a plaster cast. Old fur is rubbed off, and the base hardens into the new sheath. Horns are shed after the rut, or breeding season, in October or November. The possibility of finding such a treasure provides extra incentive to get out of the car and cover some ground on foot.

Sage lands can seem bland to those of us accustomed to more cluttered views in which big trees, blind corners, and buildings keep our minds reaching for what's over the hill, around the bend, or behind the wall. In the desert, the future waits clearly at the curve of the earth or at the foot of a mountain three daydreams away. In this huge landscape, the most beautiful views can be in a three-foot radius around your boots. Things grow close to the earth in defense against the sun and drying winds. Silvery lupine, Indian rice grass, buckwheat, and yarrow bloom and then dry into exquisite arrangements among coyote tracks, snake skins, rabbit holes, feathers, and chips of obsidian.

In the fall, groves of quaking aspen tucked into the land glow yellow and orange. The slightest breeze sets the leaves rattling. It is said that early French-Canadian trappers believed Christ was crucified on a cross of aspen and the tree hasn't quit trembling since. But probably, it has something to do with the way aspen leaves are set at right angles to their flat stems. Aspens often reproduce by sending out underground runners; so entire groves may be clones of one parent, with all the trees turning an identical color and losing their leaves in unison.

But don't look for pronghorns in the aspens. "Pronghorns," writes biologist John A. Byers in an April 1989 article in *Natural History,* "seem nervous around trees." Little wonder, as they prefer running to hiding and their unique alarm system only works in the open. Pronghorns use their rumps like signal mirrors. A patch of bright white hair fits like a hubcap over the animal's russet rear end, and when the pronghorn is alarmed, the stiff hairs bristle into a reflective disk. Darting across the sagebrush in a tight group, the pronghorns' rumps flash like schooling fish, effectively alerting sharp-eyed herds miles away. Other species, such as elk and bighorn sheep, have a light-colored rump patch, but no other animal uses the patch like a controlled device.

There's more to this hairy hubcap than meets the eye. Scent glands in the rump can release a shot of musk detectable even to humans at 400 yards. With nine additional scent glands distributed over their bodies, pronghorns are an earthy lot. They seem to invest a great deal of time depositing and inspecting scent. Males mark territorial boundaries in a deliberate and oft-repeated sequence known as SPUD. They Sniff the ground, Paw a spot bare, Urinate on the spot, and then step forward and Defecate precisely on target. Watch for SPUD spots when you're out looking for horns.

For most of the year, pronghorns live in small herds led by a dominant buck. Young males and older males without territories form bachelor groups. Territories are clearly defined and staunchly defended. Bucks routinely meet each other at their borders and march parallel down the boundary twenty feet apart, SPUDing and spraying scent from glands near their jaws. In late fall, after the rut, all the pronghorns in a region gather into larger, mixed-sex herds for part of the winter.

Flehman is another of the male's scent-centered rituals. Close

to the mating season, bucks sniff up urine left by a female to eval-
uate how close she is to estrus. Standing absolutely still, head up,
lips curled outward, his tongue moves the urine through special
ducts near his nose. The males of other animal species also engage
in flehmen.

Even though the male appears to dominate, the female usually
makes the ultimate pairing decision. Prior to the rut, females are
fickle and escape back and forth between territories. The males,
notes Byers, have mixed success holding females. Sometimes they
are able to block a doe's way, but "when an escape attempt esca-
lates into an all-out sequence of feints, blocks, sprints, and fast
turns, with the male lunging at the female, roaring his deep, guttural growl, blocking her path like a cow pony, and the female
running at top speed, her neck stretched forward, mouth open to
gulp air, it is the female that always wins.

"Sometimes she succeeds by catching the male off guard,
standing motionless for a minute or more, then suddenly sprinting
past him; sometimes her zigzags simply leave a less agile male
behind. Finally, a female pursued by a particularly ardent, agile
male can play her trump card, [which always wins] the contest;
she urinates, steps forward, waits until the male has sniffed the
urine and become temporarily frozen in flehman, then dashes
away."

Byers believes that territoriality is a good arrangement for
both male and female. He notes that "when females are surrounded by a group of males, the situation is always frantic, tense,
and probably physically dangerous. Males threaten and fight with
each other, hurriedly court females, and attempt to shepherd
them away from the group." So when females encounter increasing male attention toward the end of the summer, "the intense
harassment quickly drives them into the calm waters of a territorial
male's oceanic domain. This 'zone of tranquility' . . . provides the
freedom to continue a placid cycle of feeding and resting as
females approach estrus."

Everybody's happy. Except, of course, the odd buck out. And
even he'll forget it soon enough when the herd migrates to its
winter range to escape heavy snows.

The Sheldon National Wildlife Refuge, a sister refuge to Hart
Mountain located thirty-five miles away in Nevada, has been set

aside as pronghorn winter range. But if snows are light, pronghorns often stay the winter at Hart Mountain instead of moving
down to Sheldon. They go as far south and east as the snows push
them and usually no farther. Both refuges lie within the Great
Basin, a 200,000-square-mile area between the Sierra Nevada in
California and the Wasatch Mountains in Utah. It is "great" for
obvious reasons and a "basin" because rivers and streams flowing
into the region form lakes that have no outlet to the sea.

And no outlet in your mind, once you've been there. And
once you've been there, you can go back anytime—in the middle
of a meeting, stuck in traffic, or in the dentist's chair.

Those wise in the ways of animals say pronghorns manifest the
spirit of decisive action—the animal power to call on, they say,
when you're tied in knots or paralyzed by frustration. So untie the
knot, tune up your sense of adventure, point yourself toward Hart
Mountain, and run.

Timing Your Visit: October is a good month to visit Hart
Mountain. The rut is generally over by then, and herds have
calmed down and begun to collect in larger groups. The aspens
are turning color, days are still warm, and nights are clear and
cold.

Contact: For more information on Hart Mountain National
Antelope Refuge, contact the Refuge Manager, Sheldon–Hart
Mountain Refuges, P.O. Box 111, Lakeview, OR 97630;
(503)947-3315.

Getting There: To get to Hart Mountain Antelope Refuge from
Bend, go south on Highway 97 about 31 miles to Highway 31
and turn southeast. Take Highway 31 then Highway 395 for a
total of about 138 miles to Highway 140, just north of Lakeview.
Take Highway 140 east about 15 miles to the Plush cutoff. Plush
is about 19 miles north. Refuge headquarters is another 25 miles
to the northeast of Plush. Roads aren't marked very well, but with
a detailed map you should be able to find your way. Refuge roads
are unpaved and in varying conditions. Hart Mountain is remote;
be prepared with tools, water, warm clothing, and common sense.

Accommodations: For information on area facilities, contact the Lake County Chamber of Commerce, Courthouse, Lakeview, OR 97630-1577; (503)947-6040.

WHERE ELSE TO SEE PRONGHORNS

WASHINGTON

Pronghorns do not naturally occur in Washington. The Washington Department of Wildlife (then the Department of Game) began trying to introduce pronghorns into Eastern Washington in the mid-1940s but were unable to create self-sustaining populations. No introduced pronghorns have been seen since the late 1970s or early 1980s. Department biologists speculate that the region doesn't have a long enough spring and that elevations are too low. The higher elevation desert regions of southeastern Oregon can still be moist into July when Eastern Washington is bone dry. Another factor working against the introduced pronghorns could have been the lack of undeveloped, unobstructed rangeland.

OREGON

Soldier Creek Loop, southeastern Oregon: This loop takes you through some of the best pronghorn range in Oregon outside Hart Mountain. The road is remote and unpaved and high-clearance vehicles are recommended.

To get to Soldier Creek Loop from Burns, take Highway 78 east and then Highway 95 north to the town of Jordan Valley, right on the Idaho border. From Jordan Valley, follow the North Fork Owyhee Back Country Byway for a dip into Idaho and then south to Three Forks. Take Soldier Creek Road back to Highway 95.

For more information, contact the Bureau of Land Management, Vale District Office, 100 Oregon Street, Vale, OR, 97918; (503)473-3144. For information on area facilities, contact the Ontario Chamber of Commerce, 173 S.W. First Street, Ontario, OR 97914; (503)889-8012.

Junipers Reservoir RV Resort, south-central Oregon: You don't always have to go to the outback to see pronghorns. One viewing spot with amenities is Junipers Reservoir RV Resort. Pronghorns, as well as deer, coyotes, eagles, and other wildlife, can be seen from the campground, which is situated in a working cattle ranch. The resort closes in late October.

To get to Junipers Reservoir RV Resort from Lakeview, take Highway 140 west about 10 miles. The resort is right off the highway.

For more information, contact Junipers Reservoir, HC60, Box 1994A, Lakeview, OR 97630; (503)947-2050. For information on other area facilities, contact the Lake County Chamber of Commerce, Lakeview, OR 97630-1577; (503)947-6040.

CHAPTER 14

SALMON POWER

Kings in the Columbia at Bonneville Dam,
Washington/Oregon

They swim past the thick glass of the viewing window like art-
work on display, living sculpture cast in a magic alloy of shiny
platinum, rosy opal, and jet black obsidian. Their eyes are bright
dimes of glacier blue. Big chinook salmon—kings, as they're
rightly called—pushing their way inland to spawn and die. Coho
salmon swim behind the heavy pane too, holding steady against
the force of water rushing through the Bonneville Dam fish
ladder.

As I watch, anonymous fishy forms began to look less alike,

and individuals emerge as clearly as if they were wearing name tags. One chinook has a scar on its back cut in the shape of a sea lion bite. Another wears a rusty hook in its lip, with the bright orange lure still trailing. Two cohos, etched by vertical white net marks, hold their places in the current, neither falling back nor moving ahead. And that one—how did it lose its eye? A six-inch squawfish got turned sideways to the turbulence and blew back through the ladder like a tissue on the freeway.

With a little practice, it's easy tell the salmon species apart; chinook and coho are as different as black cottonwood and white alder. The chinook is a great, deep-bodied slab of a fish with a black gumline; its beefy tail is covered top to bottom with black spots. The coho is smaller and more streamlined, with a white gumline and spots on only the top half of the tail.

It's paradoxical that one of the best views of salmon is at a dam—a colossal, concrete bottleneck where the forces of nature ram head on into the human will—but you'd have to catch one to get any closer. In a subterranean viewing room at the Second Powerhouse of the Bonneville Dam on the Washington side of the Columbia River, five-foot picture windows spy below water level into the fish ladder. The fish ladder is less like a ladder and more like an open-air corridor filled with dinner-mint green water, speared by sunlight and carbonated by a strong current.

The Second Powerhouse viewing room is smaller and less elaborate than the viewing room across the river, but its subdued lighting and thickly padded carpets create a more intimate place to commune with kings. The Bradford Island facility on the Oregon side is the primary interpretive center, but both Bradford Island and the Second Powerhouse offer displays, films, slide shows, and bookstores.

The Bonneville Dam squats across the Columbia River forty miles east of Portland and is the first in a line of more than a dozen dams stapled across the Columbia itself. More than 100 dams control waters along the Columbia and its tributaries, which include the Snake, Cowlitz, Yakima, Spokane, Clark Fork, and Kootenay rivers.

All five species of Pacific salmon pass by Bonneville Dam at one time or another during the year, but chinook are the main attraction in the fall, when in September alone, 200,000 may be counted. Chinook salmon spend up to five years roaming the Pacific Ocean before returning to the river to spawn; coho remain in the ocean three or four years before returning to fresh water.

Each Pacific salmon species has at least two common names and varies in size. Chinook, or "kings," are the largest; they average ten to fifty pounds but are known to reach weights of more than a hundred pounds. Next in size is the chum, or "dog," salmon. Latest of the fall spawners and an important food source for wintering eagles, chums average eight to eighteen pounds. Cohos, or "silvers," and sockeye, called both "reds" and "bluebacks," are close in size and usually weigh six to twelve pounds. Pink salmon, the smallest at three to five pounds each, get their nickname "humpy" from the pronounced humps that form on the backs of spawning males.

To further complicate things, each species can be divided into a multitude of subspecies, or "runs." Hundreds of distinct runs return to specific tributaries all along the Pacific Coast. On the Columbia River, for example, three unique runs of chinook alone spawn at different times of the year—the spring, summer, and fall chinook. The Snake River's salmon runs are distinct from the Columbia River runs. The federal government has listed Snake River sockeye as an endangered species and has listed Snake River spring/summer chinook and fall chinook as threatened. So far, no Columbia River runs have been placed on the list of threatened and endangered species.

When politicians, environmentalists, fishermen, farmers, and power companies talk about endangered salmon, they are usually referring to specific runs, not whole species. Take sockeye salmon, for example. Only a few endangered Snake River sockeye returned to their Idaho spawning grounds in 1991. But in Canada and Alaska, the annual return of wild, nonhatchery sockeye salmon numbers well over 50 million fish.

In a word, dam.

The Columbia River system has been turned into a series of reservoirs, river parts, and substations. Some dams, including Bonneville, were built with fish ladders as original equipment, but most were primitive at best. Irrigation canals along the way were unscreened, and salmon could get diverted into them, ending up in alfalfa fields trying futilely to spawn in the dirt.

Grand Coulee Dam was built with no fish passage at all. That one dam alone completely shut off more than 1000 miles of river to spawning fish.

On the Snake River, hundreds of miles of spawning grounds were wiped out when Hell's Canyon Dam was built. Nearly half of the river's total fish population was destroyed. Some 100 different runs of salmon and steelhead trout have been extinguished to date from the Snake and Columbia rivers.

But in the late 1920s, fish runs weren't foremost in people's minds. The world was in turmoil, and the United States was gasping for economic breath. Bonneville Dam, a monumental project begun in 1933 and dedicated four years later by President Franklin D. Roosevelt, helped pull the country out of the Great Depression. The Grand Coulee Dam joined the flood of progress in 1941. Bonneville, Grand Coulee, and numerous other smaller hydroprojects provided the jobs, cheap power, and irrigation water that opened the Northwest. The dams are credited with helping the Allies win World War II by supplying cheap power to the shipbuilding and aluminum industries and enabling the manufacture of atomic bombs at Hanford. Today, the thoroughly tapped rivers provide about 80 percent of the region's electrical power and irrigate 3 million acres of agricultural land that feeds people around the world.

But industrial progress was made at the expense of a tremendously important fish run. Before the dams were built, 10 million to 16 million fish a year returned to the Columbia River system. Today, fewer than 2 million return. Of those, 80 percent are hatchery fish that began life in a plastic trough inside a building.

State and federal agencies, power companies, Native American tribes, and private groups spend millions of dollars on hatchery programs. The Bonneville Hatchery produces most of the hatchery fish for the Columbia River. Open to the public, the facility includes fifty-eight rearing ponds, four adult holding ponds, and its own fish ladder. In the fall, hordes of hatchery chinook make their way up the ladder and gather in concrete ponds. Dark, lusty, thirty-pound salmon crowd the raceways and take occasional running leaps at the wooden gates blocking their path. Their churning fins and backs are almost close enough to touch.

Hatchery workers collect the broodstock and remove eggs

from females and sperm from males. Fertilization is accomplished by the high-tech method of putting sperm and eggs into a bucket and stirring with a rubber-gloved hand. About 2 million coho and 26 million fall chinook fry are produced at the hatchery annually. Spawned-out fish are sold to commercial processors for smoking, canning, or turning into fish by-products. Even in a natural setting, Pacific salmon die after spawning. In the wild, fish carcasses are recycled through the bellies of eagles, bears, ravens, crows, and coyotes. Reproduction takes a huge energy toll, especially on the fish that migrate great distances inland. Some salmon travel hundreds of miles to their spawning streams.

It's not known for sure, but salmon may use currents, stars, or the earth's magnetic field to find their way from the ocean to the mouth of their home river system. From there, scientists speculate that the fish smell their way back to the exact tributary of their birth. Olfactory hints may come from the rocks, soil, or from decaying plants and animals.

As soon as salmon enter fresh water, they quit eating and subsist on stored fat. Males develop hooked snouts or humps on their backs, and both sexes change color from bright silver to red, black, or green.

Once the spawning stream is reached, the female digs a nest in the gravel by turning on her side and whisking out a depression. She deposits a few hundred eggs in the nest, called a redd, and then a male deposits sperm suspended in a milky fluid called milt. The female moves a few feet upstream and digs a new redd. The gravel she churns up in the process will cover the previous nest. The sequence continues until she has laid several thousand eggs.

Eggs hatch in the winter, and juvenile fish spend anywhere from a few months to a few years in fresh water, depending upon the species. When they begin their migration downstream toward the sea, juveniles undergo a physiological transformation that readies them for life in a marine environment. Once the process is complete, the smolt, as the young fish is now called, must get to the sea in relatively short order or it will die. As fish ladders don't work in reverse, dams complicate the out-migration for smolts as much as they complicate in-migration for adults.

Smolts swimming downstream can get sucked through a dam's turbines; 15 percent of those that go through the turbines die from radical pressure changes. Smolts that manage to avoid the turbines and spill over the dam may be so stunned by the fall that they become easy prey for birds and predatory fish. Another danger imposed by the fall comes when the smolt's gills absorb the nitrogen-rich froth in the water at the bottom. Nitrogen poisoning results in a condition similar to the bends.

In response to public sentiment and new regulations, the U.S. Army Corps of Engineers, which manages many dams in the Northwest, is investing time, effort, and money into finding and implementing safe ways for fish to pass. The Corps has stated its commitment to improving passage at dams and has taken steps that include spilling water in ways designed to minimize nitrogen supersaturation and installing "flip lips" to break smolts' falls to the base of spillways. Special fish passages and screens have also been installed in some dams to help smolts avoid turbines, and in certain situations smolts are transported around dams in trucks and barges. All these efforts have increased smolt survival rates. Considering the fact that the young fish may have to pass up to nine major dams before reaching the sea, every effort is an investment in salmon futures.

The Columbia River and its once-lavish salmon runs were at the heart of Pacific Northwest Native American culture. It has been said that Coyote created the Columbia in order to get fish over the mountains to the People.

Colville Nation storytellers say that long ago, before the river, there was a big lake covering the valley east of the Cascades. Coyote knew that salmon would come up from the ocean to be food for the People if only there were a way through. Being ambitious as well as clever, Coyote went down and dug a hole. The water flowed from the lake out to the ocean, the salmon came up the river, and the People had plenty to eat and prospered.

Many, many years later, around the time white settlers began to arrive, about 50,000 Native Americans of various tribes were living, working, and trading along the Columbia. An entire culture had evolved around the river and the salmon that came thick enough to turn the water black. Indians came from hundreds of miles away to fish and barter goods.

In his journey down the river in the fall of 1805, Captain Meriwether Lewis wrote: "The multitudes of this fish are almost inconceivable. The water is so clear that they can readily be seen at the depth of fifteen or twenty feet. But at this season they float in such quantities down the stream, and are drifted ashore, that the Indians have only to collect, split and dry them on the scaffolds."

It is estimated that before white settlement, Native Americans along the Columbia River system harvested an annual 18 million to 24 million pounds of salmon and steelhead, an oceangoing rainbow trout.

Celilo Falls, a spectacular cataract on the Oregon side of the Columbia just upriver from The Dalles, held special importance as a traditional fishing and gathering site. Naturalist John Muir visited the falls and wrote: "The vast river is jammed together into a long narrow slot of unknown depth cut sheer down in the basalt. This slot or trough is about a mile and a half long and about sixty yards wide at the narrowest place." Indian fishermen, and later whites, built tall fishing platforms over the roaring, turbulent water and used long-handled dip nets to scoop fish from the river below. When The Dalles Dam was built in 1957, the new reservoir drowned Celilo Falls. Maybe somewhere Coyote tells the story of When Man Stole Power from the River.

More than 8 million people are served by the electricity generated on the Columbia River system; power lines stitch the air over roadways like seams on a baseball. Two million fish are also powered by the river—fewer than in the past, but still more than in any other U.S. river system outside Alaska. These riverine users pay a high price for the electricity we consume so casually. Dams may be monuments to the industrial notion of progress, but buried within the unyielding structures, fish-viewing windows are bright memorials to nature's persistence.

The chinook with the orange lure trailing from her mouth scuttled past the window and out through an opening at the upstream end of the fish ladder. She had made it past sea gulls and squawfish as a smolt and past killer whales, sea lions, nets, and rods as an adult. Her connection to the power of the Columbia was clear. We humans are the ones caught up haggling over whether the Columbia is ultimately a river or the Northwest's greatest power tool.

Timing Your Visit: The fall salmon runs peak in early to mid-September, when an average of more than 200,000 chinook will pass Bonneville Dam. Run timings are influenced by weather and water conditions, so peak times may vary.

Contact: For more information on Bonneville Dam, contact the Public Information Office, U.S. Army Corps of Engineers, Portland District, P.O. Box 2946, Portland, OR 97208-2946. For information on how the runs are developing during any given week, call the Bonneville Visitor Center at (503)374-8820.

Getting There: Bonneville Dam is located about 40 miles east of Portland on the Columbia River. To get to Washington's Visitor Orientation and Fish Viewing buildings at the Second Powerhouse, take Highway 14 east along the Columbia from Vancouver, Washington.

To get to the Oregon-side Bradford Island Visitor Center and Bonneville Hatchery, take I-84 east along the Columbia from Portland to exit 40.

The Bridge of the Gods, 4 miles upriver from the dam, is the most convenient river crossing near Bonneville. A small toll is collected both ways.

Accommodations: For information on Oregon-side facilities, contact the Hood River County Visitors' Council, Port Marina Park, Hood River, OR; 97031; (800)366-3530. For information on Washington-side facilities, contact the Skamania County Visitor Information Center, P.O. Box 1037, Stevenson, WA 98648; (509)427-9811.

WHERE ELSE TO SEE SALMON

WASHINGTON
Issaquah Creek, greater Seattle area: Fall chinook, coho, and sockeye salmon spawn in Issaquah Creek, which winds through the small town of Issaquah. Nearly any bridge offers views of salmon;

there's even a restaurant overlook. The Issaquah Hatchery is open for self-guided tours, and Salmon Days are held the first full weekend in October.

To get to Issaquah from Seattle, take I-90 east.

For more information on Issaquah's salmon run or on area facilities, contact the Issaquah Chamber of Commerce, 155 N.W. Gilman Boulevard, Issaquah, WA 98027; (206)392-7024.

Dosewallips State Park, western Washington: There is no hatchery on the Dosewallips River, so fish don't bottleneck; but views can be good of fish in the river. The river flows through Dosewallips State Park on the west side of Hood Canal.

One way to get to Dosewallips State Park from Seattle is to take the downtown ferry to Winslow and then take Highway 305 around to Hood Canal Bridge. Cross the bridge and take Highway 104 until you can pick up U.S. Highway 101; then follow Highway 101 south to Dosewallips.

For more information on Dosewallips State Park, contact park headquarters, P.O. Drawer K, Brinnon, WA 98320; (206)796-4415. For information on area facilities, contact the Peninsula Tourism Council Region 8, 120 Washington Avenue, Suite 101–A, Bremerton, WA 98310; (800)433-7828.

OREGON

Oxbow Park, northwestern Oregon: Fall chinook spawn in the Sandy River, which runs through this Willamette Valley park. An annual salmon festival is held in mid-October.

To get to Oxbow Park from Portland, take Highway 26 to Gresham. The park is 8 miles farther east by way of S.E. Division and Oxbow Parkway.

For more information on the park, contact Oxbow Park, 3010 S.E. Oxbow Parkway, Gresham, OR 97080; (503)663-4708 or (503)248-5151. For information on area facilities, contact the Gresham Chamber of Commerce, P.O. Box 696, Gresham, OR 97030; (503)665-1131.

Winchester Fish Viewing Area, southwestern Oregon: Fall chinook can be seen through a viewing window as they head up the North Umpqua River.

To get to Winchester Fish Viewing Area from Roseburg, take I-5 north and exit at Winchester (exit 129).

For more information on the fish-viewing chamber, contact the Oregon Department of Fish and Wildlife, 4192 N. Umpqua Highway, Roseburg, OR 97470; (503)440-3353. For information on area facilities, contact the Roseburg Visitors and Convention Bureau, P.O. Box 1262, Roseburg, OR 97470; (800)444-9584.

CHAPTER 15

Slap Happy

Beavers on the Upper Klamath Lake Canoe Trail,
Oregon

In a lab experiment, a French biologist hung a piece of bread on a string and compared the responses of a rat, a muskrat, and a beaver. The rat and muskrat lunged at the piece of bread, trying to tear pieces from the swinging bait. The beaver chewed through the string. In another test, the same researcher wound tooth-proof wire netting around the base of a willow. The beaver stacked debris beside the tree, climbed the platform higher than the wire, and gnawed through the trunk. Beavers probably have better problem-solving skills than I did when I graduated from high school. They certainly have more ambition.

But it was planning, not lack of ambition, that kept Pat and me from shoving off into the Upper Klamath Lake Canoe Trail until after dinner. In an area where they are likely to run into people, beavers adopt a nocturnal lifestyle. So, being out at last light offers the best chance of spending a little time with one of nature's most influential, industrious, and peaceable activists.

With the exception of human beings, beavers alter the environment more than any other animal. Their principal mission in life is to ensure the presence of wetlands for themselves and, consequently, for a whole food web of other animals—from insects and birds to deer and coyotes. Beavers build dams to flood the land so they can gain watery access to the trees they use for food and building materials. The impounded water also provides beavers with a measure of safety: slow moving on land, the well-adapted aquatic mammals can move quickly in the water and so are able work in relative safety from nonhuman predators like bobcats, cougars, and coyotes.

I had reserved a rental canoe earlier in the day, and we found it tied up at the end of the Rocky Point Resort dock, stocked with paddles and boat cushions. Rocky Point is a resort in the best, sixties sense of the word, with well-used brown cabins and a little store that sells beans and marshmallows.

Skimming north up the still slough, our paddles dipped and pulled through reflected clouds. Red-winged blackbirds called from the cattails in Pan-pipe voices. The well-marked canoe trail leaves the Rocky Point dock on the far west side of Upper Klamath Lake and loops through a portion of southern Oregon's Upper Klamath National Wildlife Refuge—15,000 acres of freshwater marsh on the fringes of Klamath Lake. The marsh is home to beavers, muskrats, river otters, wood ducks, least bitterns, white pelicans, and a Noah's Ark of other species. The loop is six miles in all, with options that can either shorten or lengthen the trip.

On our left the land was firm, but on our right the thickly matted marsh floated like an image from a creation myth—like Earth Being Born on Turtle's Back. Yellow pond lilies, their leaves as big as Mexican dinner plates, lay lightly on the water's surface. Native Americans used the seeds and roots of pond lilies for food. Beavers eat them too. Some of the waxy, round flowers had been nibbled on. The largest rodent in North America and second-largest in the world, beavers also eat cattails, ferns, algae, berries, salal, and even skunk cabbage. The thirty- to sixty-pound creatures are better known, however, for their fondness for tree parts, especially the bark, twigs, and leaves of willow, alder, aspen, and birch.

Beavers can fell a five-inch-diameter tree in less than thirty minutes. Actual cutting is done with the one-inch-long lower teeth; the two-inch uppers are used to hold on. Their teeth, which never stop growing, are kept honed by use.

After a tree is down, the beaver chews off all the branches and then bucks the trunk into manageable lengths. Sometimes a pair will work together to roll big logs to the pond. Beavers don't eat the wood itself, but use the stripped logs and sticks to build their lodges and dams.

Dams, typically ten to fifty feet long and three to five feet high, are begun by securing trees into the mud of the stream bottom, parallel to the current, with the butt end facing upstream. The interlacing upper branches provide an infrastructure into which sticks and other materials can be integrated. Tires, fishing poles, rags, antlers, stolen firewood, and moose skeletons have all been found woven into beaver dams.

On the downstream side of larger dams, heavy timbers are sometimes jammed against the face to brace the structure. Holes are plastered with mud, rock, grass, and roots that beavers carry to the dam in armloads held between their chin and front paws. I'm still waiting to see one walk out of the water and up the side of a dam on its hind legs with its arms full. It happens.

The amount of land flooded by a beaver dam depends on the size of the dam and the lay of the land. The damming, flooding, and subsequent natural sedimentation of beaver ponds is thought to have begot whole geographical features, such as flat mountain valleys and large lowland meadows. Beavers stay in an area until the trees give out, and then move to new territory. Over time, sediments that otherwise would be washed down and lost from the watershed are trapped by the dams. Eventually, abandoned ponds fill in completely with rich soil.

Before beavers abandon an area, however, they often build canals to get to the trees that their ponds can't reach. They dig the canals, which can be hundreds of feet long, several feet wide, and two to three feet deep, with their clawed front paws. These aqueducts connect home pond to food source and allow the beavers to move themselves and the trees back and forth in the safety of the water. Beavers usually complete the canals before they begin downing the new supply of trees. The clever constructioneurs will even build a canal to trees uphill by using a hillside creek or seep to fashion a series of dams and ponds that, when completed, provide watery stepping-stones. Beavers drag themselves and their loads down over each dam and through each pond until they reach the main canal.

The founder of the Pony Express, Alexander Majors, was quoted as having said that beavers "had more engineering skill than the entire Corps of Engineers who were connected with General Grant's army when he besieged Vicksburg."

The Klamath Marsh is already so watery there isn't a tremendous need for dams and canals, but beavers there do form twenty-inch-wide trails that duck straight into the cover of the marsh from the slough. The canoe trail is about fifty feet wide on average—narrower in some spots, wider in others. Pat and I paddled close to the bulrushes to watch for the trails, look for beaver-chewed sticks, and listen to the stiff leaves rustle in our wake. Just below the surface, feathery plants swayed weightless. Rainbow trout—keepers—leapt out of the water at frequent intervals as soon as they figured out we weren't fishing.

Eight o'clock must have been the start of the night shift; on the hour, a buffy-cheeked beaver crossed in front of our canoe. The only thing visible was its head, which looked like a concrete block under tow. The beaver slapped its tail on the water, dove, came right back up, swam a few strokes, slapped, and dove again. The resounding slap serves warning that intruders are in the neighborhood. I assumed the beaver was a female, as they do most of the tail slapping in the family. She turned and swam straight ahead of us, slapping, diving, and swimming, each time presenting a perfect silhouette of her leathery-scaled, foot-long tail.

In water, the tail serves as a rudder or scull. On land, it

becomes extra support when the beaver sits up to chew on a tree
or when it has to walk on its hind legs because its arms are full of
construction materials. Contrary to popular myth, tails are not
used as trowels or to carry mud. The tail-as-trowel myth was per-
petuated by early American colonists, many of whom—including
trappers—held the beaver in great esteem for its industriousness
and dedication to family life.

Beavers are among the few mammals that establish long-term
monogamous relationships. Although there is minimal courtship,
beaver pairs are loyal and affectionate. They sleep curled up
together, and pairs groom each other and "talk" in conversational
tones with apparently no other purpose than to be sociable.
Family units are typically composed of two adults and two generations of offspring. Females have only one litter per year, usually
bearing two to four kits at a time. Older youngsters help with
maintenance and kit-care chores.

When they initially leave the family lodge, two-year-olds
wander the countryside building mounds of mud topped with
scent from their castor glands. These "beaver mud pies," as
they're called, are thought to convey information about sex,
age, health, and diet. Characteristically businesslike, when an
unattached male catches up to an unattached female, the two
don't make a big deal about it, but just find an unoccupied territory and set up housekeeping, going straight to work on their
dam and lodge. Established pairs continue to build mud pies
around their pond and along travel routes to establish their territorial boundaries.

Our slap-happy fellow traveler had disappeared, but as soon as
we turned the northern corner of the canoe loop, she resurfaced
in front of us and then swam around and motored fast in the
opposite direction. When we didn't turn and follow, she came
around and trailed us, zigzagging our wake. About fifty feet
ahead, a dome-shaped mass of sticks was tucked onto the marshy
shore. The lodge was about six feet tall and eleven or twelve feet
in diameter. Woven in with the sticks and branches were a two-by-
four and a length of black telephone cable. What looked like a
little sun deck was packed with mud and smoothed into the sticks
near the waterline.

Lodges may be built either out in the middle of the water or against a bank. Free-standing lodges are like artificial islands with burrows chiseled into them. Bankside lodges usually conceal burrows dug into the bank. It was hard to tell on this one because the marshland seemed too soft to support a burrow. In deep, fast-running rivers, beavers may forego building a lodge altogether and just dig a burrow into the bank.

In all cases, lodge and burrow entrances are located well underwater as a safety measure, and when the surface freezes in the winter, beavers can leave the lodge and swim around under the ice. The animal's body heat and continued activity keep lodge entrances from freezing up.

For winter food supplies, beavers, who do not hibernate, cache branches underwater. Secured by mud at the bottom of the pond, branches stay fresh and provide a continuous source of nutrition from the time the water freezes over until spring breakup. After retrieving a branch from the cache, the beaver goes back to the lodge and remains on its lower level to eat. Having eaten its meal and allowed all the water to drain from its coat, it moves up to the sleeping level.

Beavers aren't the only lodge builders in the rodent family. Muskrats also create structures in the water, although they stop short of dam building. In several ways, muskrats are scaled-down versions of beavers. In terms of size, a muskrat is to a beaver what a beagle is to a basset hound. The muskrat's smaller size coupled with the fact that it doesn't build dams means that its structures can be smaller and built of lighter materials. Muskrats build rounded lodges of mud and vegetation (no sticks) about two feet high and three feet around and also construct smaller feeding shelters about one foot high. You might see both beavers and muskrats in the same waters so, along with the size difference, a good identification clue is the tail. A beaver doesn't display its broad, flat tail when swimming, but when a muskrat swims, it holds its ratlike tail out of the water or swings it back and forth on the surface.

River otters may also be in the vicinity of beavers and muskrats. Otters don't build lodges or dams and look somewhat like huge minks. The twenty-pound animals can be three or four feet long, including the thick tail.

Like beavers, river otters and muskrats were also prized for their pelts. Shaved muskrat fur was marketed as "Hudson seal." But without a doubt, beavers bore the brunt of the centuries-long fur trade.

It has been noted by at least one historian that, applied to beavers, the fur trade would more correctly be called the fiber trade. Beaver pelts were shorn and the fine underfur felted to make into hats. Beaver hats adorned the heads of navy admirals, French lieutenants, palace guards, revolutionary soldiers, and gentlemen-about-town from at least the fifteenth to the nineteenth centuries. The use of pelts for coats and blankets was secondary. Beaver felt is still used in hat making.

The fur, or fiber, trade shifted to the New World in the 1600s, by which time beaver populations had been depleted in Europe. (They were extinct in England by the mid-1400s.) Hudson's Bay Company, with a beaver pictured prominently in the company seal, was incorporated in 1670. European demand for felt hats was insatiable, and obliging trappers expanded west in their quest for pelts.

Beavers essentially grubstaked America. The Pilgrims traded beaver furs to pay their debts in London and obtain rights to land. Later, money made on beaver skins bankrolled the first permanent settlements in nearly every state west of the Mississippi.

The invention of steel traps in the 1800s almost did beavers in, but other advances in technology saved them. With the advent of a new machine process that turned silk into felt, fashions changed and interest in beaver hats faded. But after centuries of exploitation, beavers entered the twentieth century hanging by a silk thread.

In the early 1900s new game laws were put into effect, and over time beaver populations rebuilt naturally. In areas where populations had been completely wiped out, reintroductions helped things along. Today, there are an estimated 6 million to 12 million beavers in North America.

The resolute rodents have taken up residence in Portland and Seattle, as well as near the Kennedy Center for the Performing Arts in Washington, D.C., under bridges in downtown Denver, and, of course, along the northern reaches of the Upper Klamath Canoe Trail.

It was nearly dark by the time Pat and I thought about getting back to the dock; the full moon we were counting on was hidden by heavy clouds. A sudden squall sent sharp drops of rain bouncing off the water and hissing in the bottom of our canoe. We decided to take a short-cut through the marsh, even though the land and water were just varied shades of black. I had everything in my little daypack except a flashlight and a raincoat. We bumped into two dead ends for every slough throughway, but finally managed to find the right way across. At about the time we saw the distant lights of Rocky Point, the wind let up and the rain stopped.

Back on the main waterway, we paddled steadily toward the lights and the promise of hot toddies. Closer to the resort, cabins began to appear along the shore. They all seemed to be lit with the same orange glow that comes from old lamps shining on knotty pine. Stealing slowly past one small house, we saw three older couples gathered around an upright piano. The windows were open.

"You've got the cu-test li-ttle bay-bee face," they sang. When the song was over, they all laughed and clapped. One woman patted down her man's hair and affectionately smoothed the back of his shirt. I wondered how long they had been a pair and if they slept curled up together.

Timing Your Visit: Fall is a particularly good time to look for beavers because they're more active as they gather food for the winter.

Contact: For more information on the Upper Klamath Canoe Trail, contact the U.S. Fish and Wildlife Service, Klamath Basin National Wildlife Refuge, Route 1, Box 74, Tulelake, CA 96134; (916)667-2231.

For information on canoe and kayak rentals, contact the Rocky Point Resort, 28121 Rocky Point Road, Klamath Falls, OR 97601; (503)356-2287.

Getting There: To get to the canoe trail put-in spot from Klamath Falls, take Highway 140 north along the west side of Upper Klamath Lake. In about 28 miles, look for signs to Rocky Point Resort.

Accommodations: For information on area facilities, contact the Klamath County Department of Tourism, P.O. Box 1867, Klamath Falls, OR 97601; (800)445-6728.

WHERE ELSE TO SEE BEAVERS

WASHINGTON

Wilson Creek Canyon, eastern Washington: Beavers share this canyon with coyotes, mule deer, badgers, golden eagles, and ferruginous hawks.

To get to Wilson Creek Canyon from Spokane, take Highway 2 west past Wilbur to Govan. Bureau of Land Management directions say to take the county road south of Govan about 3.5 miles to the intersection of another unmarked county road, and then go west 1 mile to the Lewis Bridge crossing of Wilson Creek. Park in the small area next to the bridge. The canyon begins just south of the bridge. A short trail leads to an overlook.

For more information on Wilson Creek Canyon, contact the Bureau of Land Management, E. 4217 Main, Spokane, WA 99202; (509)353-2570. For information on area facilities, contact the Wilbur Chamber of Commerce, P.O. Box 118, Wilbur, WA 99185; (509)647-5533.

Long Island, Willapa National Wildlife Refuge, southwestern Washington: Canoeing through the sloughs at the northern end of Long Island is as good a way as any to begin looking for beavers, which are abundant throughout the area. Since mudflats surround the island, carefully plan your time on the water around high tide.

The canoe launch is located at refuge headquarters right off U.S. Highway 101, 8 miles northeast of Seaview, Washington. The Willapa National Wildlife Refuge is about 50 miles south of Aberdeen, about 60 miles east and north of Longview, and about 25 miles north of Astoria, Oregon.

For more information on Long Island and the Willapa National Wildlife Refuge, contact the Willapa Bay National Refuge, Ilwaco, WA 98624; (206)484-3482. Seven primitive campsites are located on Long Island. For information on other area facilities, contact the Long Beach Peninsula Visitors' Bureau, P.O. Box 562, Long Beach, WA 98631; (206)642-2400.

OREGON

Tryon Creek State Park, Portland area: Visitors to this suburban park 6 miles southwest of Portland may see pileated woodpeckers and Pacific giant salamanders as well as beavers.

To get to Tryon Creek State Park from Portland, take the Terwilliger exit off I-5 and follow signs to the park.

For more information, contact Oregon State Parks, 3554 S.E. 82nd Avenue, Portland, OR 97266; (503)238-7488. For information on area facilities, contact the Portland Visitors' Association, 26 S.W. Salmon, Portland, OR 97204; (503)222-2223, or outside Oregon, call (800)345-3214.

Metro Washington Park Zoo, Portland: It may not be too wild, but the views are great and you'll learn something. The Metro Washington Park Zoo's award-winning Cascade Stream and Pond exhibit includes beavers as well as other native plant and animal species.

To get to the zoo, take Highway 26 west. The zoo is five minutes from downtown Portland. You can also take the number 63 city bus from downtown.

For more information, contact the Metro Washington Park Zoo, 4001 S.W. Canyon Road, Portland, OR 97221; (503)226-1561. For information on area facilities, contact the Portland Visitors' Association, 26 S.W. Salmon, Portland, OR 97204; (503)222-2223, or outside Oregon, call (800)345-3214.

WINTER

CHAPTER 16

SIBERIAN SNOWS

Snow Geese in the Skagit Valley, Washington

The Fir Island forecast called for flurries of snow geese. I packed binoculars, boots, gloves, and a bagful of housewarming presents for John, who had lost everything in the previous winter's flood.

Fir Island is actually a fourteen-square-mile wedge of Skagit Valley farmland situated at the end of the valley where the land meets Skagit Bay. The bay provides one border for the triangle; the other two sides are edged by the heavily diked North and South forks of the Skagit River. Along the bay edge, Fir Island is frayed by creeks, channels, streams, sloughs, and marshes. A flood plain for sure, and a veritable waterfowl paradise. Just sixty miles north of Seattle, Fir Island is ground zero for Washington's wintering snow geese.

Every fall, tens of thousands of snow geese travel through the Northwest from breeding grounds on Wrangel Island, off the northern coast of Siberia. About 26,000 geese remain all winter in Skagit Valley fields and bays. The others fly on to wintering areas in Oregon and California.

I hadn't been back to Fir Island since the previous November, when we loaded what we could of John's things into a rowboat moored to the mailbox. He had finally moved back into his place; the land had been drained and the dikes restored.

"Come on up," he said. "The geese are thick, and you won't have to carry one box of wet books."

Going to see the snow geese is a seasonal ritual. I'm never convinced winter has come to western Washington until I've seen the huge flocks gift-wrapping the Skagit Valley landscape. The Skagit River is the ribbon that ties the package together.

After the Columbia River, the Skagit is the second largest river on the West Coast outside Alaska. Every year, the river washes down 10 million tons of sediment, continually creating new land and wetlands. In the quiet waters of Skagit Bay, the river delta has advanced patiently and dependably for 10,000 years. Places like this must have seeded the original collective consciousness that commands migration instinct.

Seventy percent of Washington's tidal wetlands have been filled for development. When southbound geese, ducks, swans, and shorebirds find view apartments in place of last year's marshy stopover, I wonder if they feel lobotomized.

The Skagit Valley is, for now, shorter on pavement and longer on farm fields and state-owned wildlife lands. On Fir Island, the Skagit Wildlife Area protects 12,000 acres of habitat for snow geese and 175 other species of birds.

I left the freeway at Conway, drove west over the bridge across the South Fork of the Skagit, and turned off the radio. Clouds rumbled over the valley like a heavy bedspread; thick light worked its way through a few threadbare spots. Skagit skies build and break with great drama.

I stopped on the side of Wylie Road to watch ten swans

grazing through a stubble field. Snow geese aren't the Skagit's only big, white birds—the valley is also a winter home to nearly 2,000 swans. Wind rattled my truck, making it hard to hold the binoculars still enough to distinguish trumpeters from tundras. Trumpeter swans are the largest waterfowl in North America, weighing up to thirty pounds with wing spans up to eight feet; tundra swans are only slightly smaller. By comparison, snow geese average four to six and a half pounds.

Although the two swan species look very much alike, trumpeters have a longer neck, flatter head, and more heavily black bill. It's easier to tell them apart if they're using their voices. Trumpeters have a deep, loud call, and tundra swans, formerly called whistling swans, make a higher pitched, trilling coo. But these particular fallen angels were too busy eating to trumpet or coo, so I gave up and drove on to John's.

Thirty minutes later, John and I were in his truck, settled on the side of another road watching 12,000 snow geese puddle across the field like cold, whole milk. The edge of the close-packed flock rolled forward in a clean front. It must be winter.

Strongly flock-oriented, snow geese rarely stay in groups smaller than a hundred, and in the Skagit, crowds in the thousands are more common. Both male and female are white with jet black wing tips, and have pink feet and pink bills with a black "grin line" penned on like Halloween lipstick. On the ground, the folded wing tip is invisible except for a bit of black feather sticking out by the tail. In the air, the black wing tips are a striking contrast among the white bodies. Juveniles break the pattern by being pale gray.

grin line

Tundra and trumpeter swans and other waterfowl routinely loiter with the huge flocks of snow geese, adding multiplicity of sight and sound in crowded fields. The noise, however, is almost purely a product of the geese.

Notorious as the most persistently vocal of all waterfowl, snow geese seem to find comfort in their own voices, clamoring constantly while eating and flying. Unlike the resonant two-syllable *uh-honk* of a Canada goose, snow geese have a higher pitched one-syllable call. In spite of a cold drizzle and feather-ruffling wind, we kept the windows down and enjoyed the din. Every once in a while, an individual voice carried clearly above the rest.

After they've been here for a period of time, the geese's white heads get stained orange from probing the mud for roots and bugs.

Before agriculture came to the valley, snow geese fed on the rhizomes, or underwater roots, of aquatic grasses. Abundant wetland plants such as the three-square bulrush are what drew snow geese to the Skagit River Delta in the first place. They supplemented their diet with other grasses, marine invertebrates, and insects. As new generations of farmers cultivated the land, subsequent generations of geese cultivated new tastes for winter wheat, pasture grass, and potatoes.

Potatoes seem particularly enticing. By the time snow geese arrive in late fall, potato fields have been harvested, but mechanical harvesters leave enough behind to provide food for the geese and entertainment for goose watchers. The first snow geese I ever saw were working over a dug-up potato field. I had expected classy white ambassadors from the land of Dr. Zhivago, but what I saw was a muddy mess. The geese would scramble over the top of big dirt berms and dive for a puddle on the other side, dropping out of sight. It looked and sounded like amateur night at the mud wrestling finals.

I rolled up my window and watched the grazing flock drift across the field. Although the perimeter remained intact, small bands were constantly rising, circling, and resettling. A bald eagle dove on a corner of the flock, setting off a reactionary feathered cloudburst and twisting up the decibel level. The eagle flew off empty-taloned and the disturbed geese quickly sank back to earth.

We noticed three geese with broad plastic collars around their necks. Two of the collars were red with big, white numbers. Red collars have been used to mark a sampling of geese on their Siberian breeding grounds. I envisioned the two birds as they were being rounded up by biologists on Wrangel Island, a place of polar bears, arctic foxes, and short summers. The biologists had collared the birds, logged the numbers, and released the geese so that they could travel 3,000 miles to spend the winter eating potato bits in the Skagit Valley mud.

The third collar was brown. Brown collars have been used

by Canadian biologists to mark birds that spend time on the Fraser River Delta, an important wintering area near Vancouver, British Columbia.

Wildlife officials and amateur ornithologists keep track of collar sightings in an effort to learn more about the breeding and migratory habits of snow geese. Even after the breakup of the Soviet Union, biologists from the United States, Canada, and the former U.S.S.R. have made efforts to share information and develop strategies for snow goose management.

Earlier in this century, hundreds of thousands of snow geese toured back and forth between Wrangel Island and the Northwest. But by 1975, harsh weather during the breeding season and predation by arctic foxes had driven the Wrangel Island population down to only one colony of 45,000. Not much could be done about the weather, but modified hunting seasons in the Pacific Northwest have helped the population rebound to about 200,000.

The Wrangel Island snow geese account for only a fraction of the total snow goose population. Much larger nesting colonies exist in north-central Canada and the Canadian Arctic. Snow geese are actually the second most abundant species of goose in North America after the Canada goose.

Because Pacific Northwest populations are not as large as those farther east, the number of snow geese taken during hunting seasons in Pacific states is closely monitored. One season's take in Washington can range from fewer than 500 to more than 1,500, depending on weather and other hunting conditions. If the ratio of juveniles to adults or the overall population falls below certain levels, hunting is closed. Only two emergency closures have been necessary since 1975.

It is best to wait until after hunting season to watch the snow geese because, during the season, the birds know what's going on and tend to stay far out in Skagit and Port Susan bays. After the season closes in late December or early January, they relax and start to move into the fields to feed during the day. By mid-January, they move into the area south of Stanwood, both into the fields and along the shoreline where the Stillaguamish River flows into Port Susan. From there, they gravitate north and are soon seen in fields from Stanwood to La Conner. By late January, the best place for watching geese is Fir Island.

When I want to know where snow geese are on any given day, I call John. You'll have to drive around a bit or make friends with your own Fir Island resident. But, as the wildlife watching mantra goes, the search is half the fun. Fill your camera with film, your thermos with hot chocolate, and your car with congenial friends or family. Don't think about how the expression "wild goose chase" originated, and make a vow to end the day with dinner in picturesque La Conner. Anyway, the odds are good you won't be skunked.

Take the Conway–La Conner exit off I-5, drive straight west onto Fir Island Road, and start scanning the pastures, potato fields, and winter wheat fields. Every five minutes or so, pull over and watch the sky close to the horizon. Let your eyes adjust for dark scratches—short lines of geese coming and going from a flock. Then it's simply a matter of getting closer, staying on the road and out of farmers' backyards.

Although there are many acres of public-access wildlife lands on Fir Island, chances are the geese will be on private property. Respect the residents' privacy and property. Never assume it's okay to sit in someone's driveway or idle your four-wheel-drive around the back of a stranger's barn to have a better look. That's trespassing.

The geese, too, need respect and lots of room. Wildlife officials, landowners, and fellow bird watchers are extremely resentful of miscreants who flush snow geese for the sake of a showy photo. Stay in your car. People are known to report goose flushers and loose dogs to the game warden, who can write citations for disturbing wildlife.

For the geese, it's not merely a matter of consideration; it's a matter of life and death. Every time they're forced to fly—which is harassment—they waste precious energy and eating time. Their metabolic budget is too tight for much fooling around.

With a little patience, you'll find plenty of naturally occurring excitement to observe—like, for instance, every evening at dusk, when snow geese leave the fields for a night's safe rest on the water.

At about five o'clock, John and I stationed ourselves discreetly on the flight path between the fields and the bay. About a quarter-mile away, we could see and hear a white pancake of 2,000 geese growing restless with the dwindling light. Gusts of wind bent the grass and tangled my hair around my binoculars. Small groups of counter-commuting mallards caught in the tail wind whipped past, heading from a day on the bay to a night on inland rivers and ponds.

The falling dark tightened around the earth-bound flock like a blood-pressure cuff. The voices got louder, the sound more compact. Dusk pumped away, but the geese held firm until the last minute.

"Liftoff," said John. Platoons of geese began to rise up. One after another, they burst into the air in squalls of black-tipped wings. Each burst stacked the noise level one higher. Then the snowy cloud was low over our heads. Snow geese don't fly in neat Vs like Canada geese—they fly in flurries, sown three-dimensionally throughout the air space.

Geese were flying sideways, crabbing into the wind to keep their bearings straight. More dark ducks blasted the other way, like buckshot, through the white flock. I felt the pressure now, squeezed by the exhilaration of being with wild things at a time and place blurry enough to belong, even for just an instant. I love winter in western Washington.

Timing Your Visit: Snow geese begin to arrive in the Skagit Valley in early October, but the best viewing begins in mid-January. Large numbers of snow geese can be seen on Fir Island and in Skagit Valley fields from late January through mid-April.

Contact: For more information on snow geese in the Skagit Valley or about the Skagit Wildlife Area, contact the Washington Department of Wildlife, 16018 Mill Creek Boulevard, Mill Creek, WA 98012; (206)775-1311.

For more information on the Skagit River watershed, including cultural and geological history as well as discussions of local flora and fauna, order a copy of the booklet *From the Mountains to the Sea: A Guide to the Skagit River Watershed,* by Saul Weisberg and John Riedel of the North Cascades Institute. Contact North Cascades Institute, 2105 Highway 20, Sedro Woolley, WA 98284; (206)856-5700.

Getting There: To get to Fir Island from Seattle, take I-5 north 53 miles to the Conway–La Conner exit. Head west through Conway and you will end up on Fir Island Road. To look for geese, drive along Fir Island Road, Maupin Road, and Polson Road. The Jensen access, off Maupin Road, offers a strategic view overlooking the tidal flats if geese aren't in the fields. All roads are marked on the DeLorme *Washington Atlas and Gazetteer.*

Accommodations: A bed-and-breakfast stay is a great way to consummate the snow goose winter ritual. For information on La Conner facilities, contact the La Conner Chamber of Commerce, P.O. Box 644, La Conner, WA 98257; (206)466-4778.

WHERE ELSE TO SEE SNOW GEESE

WASHINGTON

Willapa National Wildlife Refuge, southwestern Washington: In Washington, wintering snow geese are found only in and around the Skagit Valley. You can, however, find wintering swans and tens of thousands of other wintering waterfowl at the Willapa National Wildlife Refuge. Both trumpeter and tundra swans use the area, as do black brant and common and arctic loons.

The Willapa National Wildlife Refuge is located about 50 miles south of Aberdeen. Refuge headquarters sits right off U.S. Highway 101, 8 miles northeast of Seaview, Washington. The Riekkola Unit of the refuge, accessible by Yeaton Road from Long Beach, contains pastures and freshwater marshes. Roads are open to foot travel and offer good views of waterfowl.

For more information about the refuge or about winter viewing opportunities, contact the Willapa Bay National Wildlife Refuge, Ilwaco, WA 98624; (206)484-3482. For information on area facilities, contact the Long Beach Peninsula Visitors' Bureau, P.O. Box 562, Long Beach, WA 98631; (206)642-2400.

OREGON

Lower Klamath National Wildlife Refuge, south-central Oregon: Established in 1908 by President Theodore Roosevelt, Lower Klamath National Wildlife Refuge was the nation's first waterfowl refuge. Like an iceberg, only the tip of the refuge is in Oregon; most of the 47,600 acres are south of the state line in California. But what's a little thing like state boundaries to a few thousand Siberian geese?

To get to Lower Klamath National Wildlife Refuge from Klamath Falls, drive south on Highway 97 for about 19 miles and turn east into the refuge on Highway 161, which runs along the California–Oregon Border. To get to refuge headquarters, located east of the refuge in California, turn south off Highway 161 onto Hill Road and go about 4 miles.

For more information on Lower Klamath National Wildlife Refuge, contact the Refuge Manager, Klamath Basin National Wildlife Refuges, Route 1, Box 74, Tulelake, CA 96134; (916)667-2231. For information on area facilities, contact the Klamath County Department of Tourism, P.O. Box 1867, Klamath Falls, OR 97601; (800)445-6728.

Summer Lake Wildlife Area, southeastern Oregon: Klamath Basin is the only area in Oregon that can claim any real numbers of wintering snow geese. But snow geese do migrate through the state in huge numbers. At Summer Lake, an average of 70,000 to 80,000 snow geese pass through in the fall and spring. Many of these geese are from Canadian nesting areas. The best time to see snow geese at Summer Lake is in the first two weeks of November or first two weeks of March.

Summer Lake is also notable for its trumpeter swan project. In the fall of 1991, wildlife officials transplanted 100 trumpeter swans from Harriman Lake in Idaho in an effort to encourage the swans to establish a winter home there.

To get to Summer Lake from Bend, take Highway 97 south to LaPine. Just south of LaPine, take Highway 31, heading southeast, to the town of Summer Lake. The lake is a few miles beyond town.

For more information on snow geese at Summer Lake, contact Oregon Department of Fish and Wildlife, Box 8, Hines, OR 97738; (503)573-6582. For information on area facilities, contact the Lake County Chamber of Commerce, P.O. Box 616, LaPine, OR 97739; (503)536-9771.

CANADA

George C. Reifel Waterfowl Refuge, Delta, British Columbia: Over the Canadian border just south of Vancouver, British Columbia, the George C. Reifel Waterfowl Refuge is as important to wintering snow geese as is the Skagit Valley. Twenty thousand to 30,000 snow geese and hundreds of swans winter in the refuge which is located at the mouth of the Fraser River. Numbers peak in November, and viewing is excellent through December.

To get to the George C. Reifel Wildlife Refuge from Vancouver, B.C., take Highway 99 south through the George Massey Tunnel to the Ladner cutoff. Drive west of Ladner to the Westham Island Bridge and follow signs to the refuge. Check at refuge headquarters for trail maps and an updated sightings list. There is an entrance fee.

For more information on the refuge, contact George C. Reifel Waterfowl Refuge, 5191 Robertson Road, Delta, B.C., Canada V4K 3N2; (604)946-6980. For information on facilities in the greater Vancouver area, contact the Tourism Association of Southwestern B.C., #304 -828 W. 8th Avenue, Vancouver, B.C. Canada, V5Z 1E2; (604)876-3088.

CHAPTER 17

BIG-EARED DEER

Mule Deer in the Methow Valley, Washington

The old wooden sign leaned out of a snowdrift next to the road: *"Entering Methow Wildlife Area—Pardners in Progress."* It's nice when public agencies and private interests refer to each other as pardners, and progress means more deer, not more development.

The narrow lane disappearing into the evergreens was tucked under a thick cover of wet snow and looked impassable, although Pat, who has a tendency to push his luck, was willing to give it a try. This wasn't the only entrance into the wildlife area, but it was the best way into Beaver Creek—a favorite wintering spot for a good share of Methow Valley's 20,000 mule deer. In a place where you have to try hard not to see deer, we hadn't seen one all morning.

The greater Methow Valley contains hundreds of square miles of usable winter range—a mix of low-elevation open space and cover where deer can find food and shelter during the cold months. In the summer, Methow deer spread out into the mountainous, roadless country of the Pasayten Wilderness or wander up the slopes that divide Methow Valley from Lake Chelan to the west. In the fall, heavy snows in the high country push deer back down into the valley, where they remain for the winter.

We had originally planned to ski into the wildlife area. The Methow Valley is usually a wonderland for cross-country skiers, but like many other places in the Northwest, winter had been abnormally stingy with its snowfall. In place of January's typical layers of fresh, fluffy, ski snow, the ground was covered with crusted mush over mud. We decided to walk in.

Forgetting the first rule of the woods—silence—we banged out of the van, charging around finding hats and gloves and trying to decide which boots to wear. We had been shouting at each other across the vehicle for five minutes when Pat started waving his hands at me and tapping his lips with his finger. Right.

Just behind the wildlife sign, a mule deer doe stood with her two fawns, watching us. They were a vignette of winter loveliness, framed in the sun and shadow of the snowy forest. The doe's seven-inch-long ears twitched up and forward.

Lewis and Clark first used the term "mule deer"—undoubtedly a nod to the species' ample ears and large size. In fact, ears are often the first thing you see of deer in heavy cover; the animal takes form around its ears like the Cheshire cat around its smile.

Hanging behind their mother, the two fawns were about a quarter smaller, except for their ears, which were nearly as big as the doe's. Fawns grow into their ears the way puppies grow into their paws. All three had fluffed out their thick, sandy brown coats for warmth.

With calm, cautious grace, the doe approached the barbed-wire fence separating the road from the woods. The young ones stayed back. Without even an extra breath, she sproinged over the fence, taking off and landing on all fours. *Cush cush cush cush.* She trotted through the soft, wet snow to the edge of the trees on the other side. The fawns waited one more minute and walked up to the fence. We waited for them to jump. They gathered themselves up—then popped straight through a gap in the fence where the wire bowed like horizontal barbed parentheses. Regrouped, the family disappeared.

Availability of suitable land on which to spend the winter has become a common limiting factor for twentieth-century wildlife. The kind of habitat that makes good winter range—low elevation, protected southern exposures, relatively moderate temperatures, productive soil, and accessible water—also makes good house sites, orchards, alfalfa fields, golf courses, apartment complexes, and shopping malls. When winter range is reduced by development, too many animals crowd into the small area left over. Habitat is trampled and food plants are overgrazed, jeopardizing the long-term ability of the land to support wildlife.

In the case of deer, a certain amount of habitat alteration can be beneficial. For instance, selective logging, where only a portion of the trees in a stand are cut, opens the canopy and allows the understory vegetation to flourish. Deer thrive on the huckleberry, salal, vine maple, and alder that grow in these openings. Clearcuts are a different matter. Regrown clearcuts are good places to find deer, but the initial disturbance and total removal of vegetation associated with clearcut logging leaves an area unsuitable for deer and most other wildlife for several years.

From where we stood at the Beaver Creek entrance to the wildlife area, the cold-water-over-rocks sound of the creek was all we could hear. No trucks, no planes, no snowmobiles. No disturbance. Even the latest deer seasons are over by mid-December, and although people are allowed to shoot coyotes all winter, no rifle shots troubled the silence. We followed a braid of deer tracks down the road and into the woods. Vegetation was heavy on both sides of the creek, which really does have a beaver living on it in a quiet, snow-covered lodge.

Following a deer trail is a walking meditation. The subconscious brain kicks in to take over the mechanics of walking, freeing the mind to notice such things as lightly shed deer hairs, lying across the snow like Chinese calligraphy.

Deer and humans have a long history of coexistence. Deer

skins provided shelter and clothing for early peoples; antlers and bones became buttons and tools. Deer meat kept families alive through the winter. The seasonal deer hunt is still an important tradition for many people.

In return, humans cleared the forests and planted crops, allowing some deer populations to grow. The time came, however, when too much land was converted to human use, and deer numbers began to decline. Still, experts believe there are more deer today than there were when Europeans first arrived. Early nineteenth-century settlers at Fort Okanogan ate more horse than venison.

The Washington Department of Game (now the Department of Wildlife) first purchased Methow Valley land to set aside as mule deer winter range in 1939. The most recent purchase, in 1991, brings the total wildlife area to 23,045 acres, distributed among four separate units. The 14,000-acre Methow Unit, largest of the four, lies east of Highway 20 in a rough crescent paralleling the Methow River between Winthrop and Twisp. Although mule deer are the most abundant type of deer in the area, white-tailed deer can also be found here, especially in bottomland near the river.

Three species of deer are found in Washington: mule deer, black-tailed deer, and white-tailed deer. The black-tailed deer, most abundant of Washington's estimated 400,000 deer, is considered a subspecies of mule deer and lives only west of the Cascade Mountains. Mule deer are Washington's second-most abundant species and can be found all the way from the eastern slopes of the Cascades through the sage plains and wheat fields of eastern Washington. White-tailed deer, common to the lowland forests and brushlands of the eastern and central United States, are found on both sides of the Cascades.

Columbian white-tailed deer, one of thirty-eight subspecies of white-taileds, once ranged from south Puget Sound to Roseburg, Oregon. Primarily because of habitat loss, these deer are now listed as endangered in both Oregon and Washington. Establishment of a Columbian white-tailed deer refuge in southwestern Washington and implementation of an effective management plan have succeeded in helping the population rebound.

Telling deer apart is largely a heads-or-tails proposition. Ears, antlers, and tails provide the three most obvious clues, although antlers are useful only for identifying males, and only during certain months. Females don't grow antlers, and bucks shed theirs every year in the late winter, with new growth beginning in April or May. (Of all the antlered animals, only caribou females grow antlers. Among animals with horns instead of antlers—such as bighorn sheep, mountain goats, and bison—both male and female grow horns.)

Bambi must have been a white-tailed deer. When those deer run, their big tails wave like the white glove on an Apple Blossom Queen. Black-tailed deer also sometimes hold their tails erect when running, but the tails are markedly smaller and don't produce the signature wave. Although the underside of a black-tailed's tail is white, the top is totally black. Muleys keep their brown tails tucked down when they run, and just the tip of the top of the tail is black.

White-tailed deer run in a conventional fashion, but mule deer and sometimes black-tailed deer can be seen springing across the ground with all four feet leaving and hitting the earth at the same time. Stotting, as this gait is called, is thought to save energy and is also useful in putting obstacles between the deer and a predator in pursuit. Nineteen-hundred-pound bison occasionally stot too, a sight worth driving across three states to see.

While it may be difficult to make a study of deer tails or stotting, antlers are another matter. Stop at any rural tavern, coffee shop, or motel where they don't serve light beer or espresso (this is getting harder to do), and chances are good there will be a deer head on the wall. Head mounts may not be your cup of cappuccino, but they do offer excellent opportunities to study antler form. Unless, of course, they are obscured by baseball caps or other ornaments.

Mule deer and black-tailed deer have antlers that branch and then rebranch—in other words, the branches branch. White-tailed deer, however, grow one main beam from which singular branches, or "points," grow. For either species, the accepted "point size" vernacular counts only the number of branches on one side. A "four-point buck" has four tines per side. In some places back East, the same buck may be called an "eight-pointer."

Walking through the wildlife area, we kept our eyes open for cast-off antlers. They're hard to find intact because rodents like to gnaw them for the calcium and other nutrients they offer.

Shed antlers aren't the only things deer leave as proof of their existence. The path we followed was strewn with scat. Deer droppings come in a variety of forms, depending on the season, size of the deer, and, naturally, what it's been eating. In spring and summer, when forage is succulent, deer scat looks like caked-together milk duds. Drier winter browse results in drier, scattered pellets.

The signs an animal leaves behind—tracks, scat, or tufts of hair or fur—lend a fourth dimension to walks in the woods. We are presented with evidence that animals exist in time and space even if we don't see them in the flesh. Like, when you trip across a log, you know a tree fell in the forest even if you didn't hear it. Being about as philosophically sophisticated as a K-Mart, these thoughts made me so dizzy I had to lie down in the deer bed I found pawed out under a tree. Deer beds are hard to resist. In the woods, they look like little rooms under the trees or in the bushes. In open fields, they look like UFO landing pads—oval spaces trampled down in the grass. Lying in a deer bed in the middle of the woods is really not the most efficient way to look for deer, but it's a lovely dalliance. In too short a time, the cold worked its way into my still bones and pushed me on.

Pat was waiting at the beaver lodge. We cut up to the road, followed an 18-inch-long red, white, and black pileated woodpecker back to the van, and turned toward more open spaces.

In the winter, deer are generally active most of the day. They collect on south-facing slopes in the same inevitable way lint collects on navy blue wool. Snow melts off the south slopes first, exposing grass and other edibles.

Winter, when individual bands may gather on prime feeding grounds, is the only time deer concentrate in large numbers. During most of the year, they move around in small, segregated groups. Three typical winter groupings are single does with one or two generations of offspring, fraternal groups of mature males, and what are called "experimental" groups composed of young deer of both sexes that are newly or temporarily on their own.

Driving across open ground back toward Twisp from Beaver Creek, we saw a gang of ravens sitting on a brown heap that, upon inspection, turned out to be a dead deer. The carcass had been there for some time, and its ribs, skin, legs, and scattered hair had already begun to recycle their elements. A big pile of coyote scat marked the spot. Winter has as many excuses for death as it has dead bodies. We had already seen three other piles of remains.

Predation by cougars and the occasional coyote, starvation, poachers, vehicles, and natural accidents such as fires, falls, and drowning all kill deer. People's pet dogs chase deer to exhaustion and then run them into fences. But the overriding influence on the Methow Valley's winter deer populations is weather. Heavy snows late in the season, or a constant, deep snow cover and cold temperatures, can spell disaster.

Ironically, many deer who make it through the winter die of malnutrition in the spring, surrounded by green grass. Deer alter their diet with the season, and as their food sources change, the bacteria in their digestive systems adjust accordingly. In hard winters when few green plants are available, the type of bacteria that digests woody plants flourishes. When grass comes back, deer fill their bellies before their systems have had a chance to reestablish the proper digestive bacteria. As a result, the grass doesn't metabolize, but deer keep eating until they die of starvation and digestive tract complications.

Nobody ever said nature was benign. Beautiful, for sure, but sometimes beastly. On the positive side, deer carcasses feed a winter-hungry host of birds, mammals, insects, and the soil itself.

Annual winterkill and the take during legal hunting seasons may have the most visible effects on deer populations, but in the long run, loss of habitat, especially winter range, will be what kills the most deer. In the decade after the North Cascades Highway (Highway 20) was completed in 1972, the human population doubled—even though this northern through-route from western to eastern Washington is closed in the winter. An environmental impact statement filed on the proposed Early Winters Ski Resort in the Methow Valley predicted the population would increase another 40 percent if the resort were built. Construction was to be adjacent to winter range and would have blocked spring and fall migration corridors. Legal maneuvering and resistance from environmentalists delayed the project for years, until the original developer ran out of money and sold the property. As of this writing, the new owners have yet to state their intentions. Local opinion on proposed development is mixed. So far, no one has discovered a single prescription for both economic growth and environmental purity.

For now, mule deer have a clear path to come and go, and the small towns of Winthrop and Twisp aren't marketing tools, but are still places where "time-share" most often means lingering over dinner with friends and family.

Pat and I used the excuse of poor snow to putter around the towns. We bought juice and licorice in a general store and searched for a public library. Our timing was right, and we found the Twisp Community Library—one room in an old wooden building—open. Near the check-out desk, a little boy was dropping live worms into a murky aquarium that housed a five-inch-long catfish another kid had caught in some secret fishing hole. He was asking the librarian questions about how fish breathe. This boy gets to learn his life's lessons on deer trails, in creek bottoms, and in the nurturance of a one-room library with a resident catfish. We should all be so lucky.

Timing Your Visit: December through February are the best months to look for deer in the Methow Valley Wildlife Area. The last deer-hunting seasons are over by mid-December.

Contact: For more information and maps of Methow Valley Wildlife Area, contact the Washington Department of Wildlife, P.O. Box 850, Ephrata, WA 98823; (509)754-4624.

Getting There: The Methow Wildlife Area is divided into several different units scattered on both sides of Highway 20 (the North Cascades Highway) between Winthrop and Twisp. Highway 20 closes between Ross Lake and Mazama with the first heavy snowfall in the winter and is not usually reopened until Memorial Day. So, to get to Beaver Creek from Wenatchee, take Highway 97 north about 56 miles and then take Highway 153 north to the Highway 20 junction 2 miles south of Twisp. Go east on Highway 20 about 5 miles to Beaver Creek Road and turn north. The wildlife area entrance is a couple of miles up Beaver Creek Road.

Off the main roads, side routes may be plowed but primitive. Be aware that a road that is firm in the morning may not be so solid after a few hours of sunshine. Use your judgment. If you'd rather not deal with the back roads, you can still see deer from paved roads or ski trails.

Accommodations: For information on area facilities, contact the Twisp Chamber of Commerce, P.O. Box 686, Twisp, WA 98856; (509)997-2926.

Where Else to See Wintering Deer

Washington
Columbian White-tailed Deer National Wildlife Refuge, southwestern Washington: This small refuge of Columbia River bottomland was established to protect the endangered Columbian white-tailed deer. Parts of the refuge are closed to public access, but a road along the perimeter provides views from which deer may be seen.

To get to the Columbian White-tailed Deer National Wildlife Refuge from Longview, take Highway 4 west to Steamboat Slough Road. Turn west on Steamboat Slough into the wildlife area.

For more information, contact refuge headquarters, P.O. Box 566, Cathlamet, WA 98612; (206)795-3915. For information on area facilities, contact the Tourist Regional Information Program, P.O. Box 876, Longview, WA 98632; (206)425-1211.

W. T. Wooten Wildlife Area, southeastern Washington: Set in the Tucannon River valley of the Blue Mountains, this remote wildlife area provides winter range for both deer and elk.

To get to the W. T. Wooten Wildlife Area from Clarkston, take Highway 12 west through Pomeroy. Just past Zumwalt, take Highway 126 as it forks left. Go south along the Tucannon River to the wildlife area.

For more information, contact the Washington Department of Wildlife, 8702 N. Division Street, Spokane, WA 99218; (509)456-4082. For information on area facilities, contact the Pomeroy Chamber of Commerce, P.O. Box 947, Pomeroy, WA 99347; (509)843-1595.

OREGON

Wallowa Lake, northeastern Oregon: Look for wintering mule deer on the south end of the lake near Wallowa Lake State Park.

To get to Wallowa Lake from La Grande, take Highway 82 east through Enterprise and Joseph to Wallowa Lake. The state park is on the south end of the lake.

For more information, contact the Wallowa Valley Ranger Station, Route 1, Box 83, Joseph, OR 97846; (503)432-2171. For information on area facilities, contact the La Grande–Union County Chamber of Commerce, 1502 N. Pine, La Grande, OR 97850; (503)963-8588.

Oatman Flat Deer-viewing Area, southeastern Oregon: Up to 1000 mule deer gather in this alfalfa pasture during the winter. Mornings and evenings are the best times to see them.

To get to Oatman Flat from Bend, take Highway 97 south to Highway 31 and follow Highway 31 south for about 39 miles to the field at the junction of Highway 31 and the Forest Service road. There are no facilities; viewing is from the edge of the road.

For more information, contact the Oregon Department of Fish and Wildlife, 61374 Parrell Road, Bend, OR 97702; (503)388-6363. For information on area facilities, contact the LaPine Chamber of Commerce, P.O. Box 616, LaPine, OR 97739; (503)536-9771.

CHAPTER 18

EAGLES EN MASSE

Bald Eagles at Bear Valley, Oregon

6:15 A.M.: It's dark, but I can see my footprints in the frost on the road. Somewhere ahead a few hundred bald eagles are waking up and thinking about leaving their communal night roost for a day of bopping ducks, scavenging swans, and chasing ground squirrels across farm fields in the Klamath Basin of south-central Oregon. The roost is in a stand of old-growth forest on a hillside half a mile away.

6:40 A.M.: A rooster has been crowing for fifteen minutes, but there's no sign of our national symbol. Bald eagles are said to be sound sleepers. Snow falls on my face cold and delicate as the fingers of a young ghost.

6:45 A.M.: Still no eagles. Near the horizon, white cracks open in the pewter stratus, and an owl hoots up dawn.

I know the eagles are there. Bear Valley National Wildlife Refuge holds one of the largest bald eagle winter roosts in the Lower 48 states, and I'm standing directly between it and five waterfowl refuges that spread like a bird-of-prey buffet table across the basin. The eagles are here because of the ducks; the ducks are here because of the refuges.

I'm here because of the fly-out—the first slice of morning when eagles flow steadily, one after another, from night roost to feeding grounds. Behind me, van doors slide open and boots scrape over frozen gravel. Smells of sage, cows—and coffee—rise with the growing light. The Klamath Basin Audubon Society has set up a card table and is selling hot drinks and homemade muffins to the hundred or so people now lining the road.

Eagles fly out from night roosts every winter day from November through February, and on a typical morning it would be just me and maybe a few other eagle watchers. But the 13th Annual Bald Eagle Conference is being held this mid-February weekend, so there is company. The conference, timed to coincide with the peak presence of eagles and waterfowl, provides a forum in which lay people and experts can share information and increase awareness of eagles and other wildlife resources—and have a good time, to boot.

A coyote just ran across the stubble field on the left, but still no eagles.

6:48 A.M.: Two jack rabbits want to cross the road from the coyote field to a stand of dark green juniper on the other side, but there are eagle watchers in the way. It's light enough now to clearly see the hillside where the roost is.

6:50 A.M.: Seven hundred feet up, a lone bald eagle heads cross-county—the epitome of independence. I shivered. Forty pairs of binoculars and at least that many pointing fingers follow its progress, and we wait another minute before the next one flies over. The tempo picks up, and thirty minutes later a woman with a thick, brown braid has counted 97. By 7:45, about 170 bald eagles—plus a generous assortment of the hawks and golden eagles who share the roost—have overflown the convivial crowd.

By 8:00 A.M. the eagles that are going are gone. Some, full enough from yesterday's outing, won't leave the roost at all today. The others will be back late in the afternoon. People disperse to attend workshops or watch birds in an area Roger Tory Peterson has called one of the nation's best birding spots.

Of the five major eagle roosts scattered around the edge of the Klamath Basin, the one in Bear Valley is the largest. Up to 300 eagles may use it at one time. A "roost" can be one tree or many, depending on the number of birds and the supply of suitable branches. The availability of a good night roost is as essential to wintering eagles as is the presence of food. Roost criteria are specific: the trees must have branches big enough to support the nine- to fifteen-pound birds, must be open enough for take-offs and landings, and must be sheltered from prevailing weather.

roosting eagles

Bear Valley is so important to the long-term survival of the Klamath Basin's wintering bald eagles that it has been set aside as a national wildlife refuge specifically to protect the roost.

Eagles are truly communal only in the winter, when they gather in groups of 12 to more than 3,000. Biologists believe that group living helps single birds find mates and is also a time for immature birds to learn survival skills. Inexperienced eagles follow adults into the field to learn how to make do when fish, the preferred food, isn't available. Although they're masterful hunters, eagles are greater opportunists, getting most of their meals by scavenging and stealing from other birds-of-prey.

The largest wintering concentration of bald eagles in North America is on the Chilkat River flats near Haines, Alaska. Thirty-five hundred eagles gather there to feed on the remains of a late run of chum salmon. In the Lower 48, the Klamath Basin claims the largest concentration, with 1,100 bald eagles. The ducks, as I mentioned, are the draw.

Hundreds of thousands of waterfowl winter in the basin, and it's normal for several thousand to die of disease or injury during the season. Dead and dying ducks, geese, and swans make it relatively easy for the eagles—who aren't susceptible to most common waterfowl diseases—to make a living.

Though the fly-out is fun to see, it's not necessary to get up in the dark to see eagles in the Klamath Basin—they're everywhere, especially in the Lower Klamath refuge, where up to 700 may pass the day. As I was driving a dike road across one of the marshes, a huge adult blasted up from the ditch, filling my windshield like a brown breaker. It curled the black talons of its big, yellow feet tight and shot me a nasty look over its shoulder. But bald eagles always look pissed; I think it's the way their fine head feathers shade a frown over those piercing, parchment-colored eyes. An eagle's gaze is searing and doesn't miss a detail.

Standing among regal white swans and crowds of simple-hearted ducks, bald eagles stick out like gangsters at a kiddie parade. They loiter among the ducks and geese, looking slick-backed and nonchalant, preening bits of duck down off their talons. The pragmatic waterfowl generally ignore their presence, because an eagle on the ground isn't hunting and therefore poses little threat. Watching an eagle standing on what looked like a broken feather pillow, I was more fixated on the scene than were the dead swan's brethren grazing indifferently twenty feet away. When the eagle couldn't raise its head high enough to pull free a beakful of guts, nobody flinched but me. Business as usual. Within minutes, other eagles were circling and landing, waiting for a turn at the carcass.

The air space in the Klamath Basin is a continuous chaos of flying forms. Lines, Vs, flocks, and dots are flying in all directions, at varying speeds, altitudes, and urgencies. Trumpeter swans fly so low over the road that you can hear the vibration of air against wing feathers. Cliques of gulls shift from one watering hole to the next like conventioneers at cocktail hour. Eagles hang out on the ground, or cruise above: flap-flap-flap-flap, gliiiiiide. Flap-flap-flap-flap, gliiiiiide.

With wingspans of up to eight feet, eagles are built to soar. All their hollow bones put together weigh less than half the total weight of their feathers. They are masters at finding and riding thermals—rising columns of heated air. The last birds to leave the roost in the morning, after the sun has been up awhile, may circle up on a thermal to gain altitude before heading out. But soaring is just for saving energy—eagles are aggressive and dexterous fliers when they want to be. They chase down their own prey, or swoop on osprey and other birds until those birds drop what they've caught for themselves. Eagles also engage in midair power plays with each other and with other birds of prey. The eagle on the defensive will roll over to display its talons to the aggressor, and sometimes the two will momentarily lock talons and tumble toward the earth before pulling out of the dive.

Flying physiology favors immature eagles. Because their tail feathers are about 23 percent longer than the tail feathers of adults, they can circle tighter and catch smaller thermals. Juveniles also have longer wing feathers, which allow for slower flight. Birds aren't born expert fliers, and slower speeds help awkward youngsters avoid crash landings.

During the cold months, eagles conserve energy by spending less time in the air. This is what makes them so easy to observe in the Klamath Basin. Instead of watching black swashes in the sky, you see eagles thirty feet away—standing, eating, hunting, wading in shallow water, even sitting down in the grass like chickens on a nest. If you can find a field that is just being flooded by irrigation equipment, pull over and watch the eagles gather to pick off the mice and ground squirrels running for high ground.

The smaller birds of prey in the Klamath Basin spend a larger percentage of their time hunting than do the bald eagles. Golden eagles (slightly smaller than balds), red-tailed hawks, rough-legged hawks, kestrels, northern harriers, and barn owls (who, unlike many other owls, fly during the day) are all visible winter residents.

Bird of prey, or raptor, identification can be tricky, even for experienced bird watchers. Not only are there many species, but among hawks and falcons there are also "morphs"—seemingly arbitrary variations of color and plumage patterns—to reckon with. But if you're the type of person who has taken the trouble to learn the difference between a 747 and a DC-10, raptor watching may be for you.

For those types of us who push past life's little details, thank goodness for adult bald eagles. With their dark brown bodies and bright white heads and tails, they offer an opportunity to identify at least one raptor with absolute certainty. Immature bald eagles, which in some years may comprise 25 percent of the bald eagle population in the Klamath Basin, are another matter.

Bald eagles start life in a plain brown plumage. Second-year birds are mottled with white under the wings and on the back and belly, and by three years, the head is turning white but still has brown flecks. Birds usually display full adult plumage in their fourth or fifth year, when the head and tail become totally bald—a word which originally meant "white."

Immature bald eagles are often confused with golden eagles. Adult goldens are uniformly dark brown with a trace of white at the base of the tail. Juveniles have large, white wing patches and a bright white banded tail, but no other white on the body. If the eagle in question has large amounts of white on it, particularly on the underside, call it an immature bald.

Bird watchers note that it's easier to turn hawks into eagles than eagles into hawks. If it's an eagle, you *know* it. If it indeed is a hawk, the first inclination is to turn it into a red-tailed hawk. Not a bad guess, because red-taileds are the most common and widespread hawks in the Northwest. But rough-legged hawks hold their own in the numbers game around the basin, so don't be too hasty.

Adult red-tailed hawks are easy to identify when the light shines just right on the red top side of the tail. Most of the seven different morphs have some red in the tail. Immature birds don't have the color signature. Generally speaking, rough-legged hawks are lighter in color than red-taileds and have dark bellies and dark wrist patches. Roughs are only slightly less complicated: they have only two morphs, but each has three plumage types.

Don't feel bad if you decide hawks are too much trouble to learn. A certain Oregon Fish and Wildlife commissioner is not embarrassed to admit that on road trips with her husband, they simply count "big birds."

By late March, most of the Klamath Basin's bald eagles are heading for home territories in Canada. Eagles form long-term pair bonds and use the same nest site every year. During the reproductive season, pairs will defend a half-mile area around the nest.

The only territory to defend in winter is a favorite perch in a roost. Older, more aggressive birds demand the highest branches and the spots nearest the trunk. The biggest territorial drama associated with the Bear Valley roost involved human beings: those who wanted to cut trees and those who wanted to save them. The battle was contentious, but local conservationists knew the outcome was critical to the wintering well-being of Klamath Basin eagles. The dispute was put to rest when, in 1978, the area was designated a national wildlife refuge. Acquisitions in 1991 brought the total area of the refuge up to 4,198 acres. Bear Valley is the only Klamath Basin refuge not managed primarily for waterfowl.

The Lower Klamath National Wildlife Refuge, established in 1908 by President Theodore Roosevelt, was the nation's first waterfowl refuge. The six refuges in the Klamath Basin complex— Lower Klamath, Upper Klamath, Clear Lake, Tule Lake, Klamath Forest, and Bear Valley—encompass a total area of 151,375 acres (some of which are in California) and include marshes, lakes, grassy meadows, coniferous forests, agricultural lands, sagebrush and juniper uplands, and rocky slopes and cliffs. More than 400 species of wildlife have been identified in the region, including most of the avian glamour species, such as trumpeter swans, peregrine falcons, and, of course, bald eagles.

But, as with many of the most magnificent species of bird, the bald eagle has suffered some inglorious moments in human history. At the same time the signatories of the Declaration of Independence were adopting the bald eagle as our national symbol, the birds were being shot as varmints and fed to the hogs. Tales of eagles carrying off piglets and lambs were greatly exaggerated. As recently as 1952, the state of Alaska paid a two-dollar bounty for every pair of "American eagle" legs turned in, even though most of the salmon that eagles eat are dead, not alive.

Before European settlement, bald eagles were common along every major river and lake shore in the continental United States. But by the early 1900s, these sanctioned symbols of strength and virtue had all but disappeared from sea to shining sea. After World War II, the already-reduced bald eagle populations were hit by a less-discriminating killer, DDT. Populations hit an all-time low when eagles began ingesting the insecticide by eating prey species in which DDT had accumulated. In 1976, the Pacific States Bald Eagle Recovery Team was established to draft a management plan for bald eagles on federal land in Oregon, Washington, California, Idaho, Montana, Nevada, and Wyoming. It took the team ten years, but a plan was finally drafted and approved.

With a management plan in place and DDT out of the picture at least in this country, populations are rebuilding. A small number of eagles are beginning to settle in large urban parks. But even viewed from a condominium window, eagles present themselves as above it all—incarnations of wildness and freedom.

An estimated 861 pairs now nest in the Northwest. As a result, there is talk of having the status of the birds changed from endangered to threatened throughout the northwestern United States. We humans learn so slowly and forget so quickly that the thought of downlisting, with its concomitant weakening of protections, makes many conservationists nervous.

I wouldn't mind seeing protections for all vulnerable species remain in place until there are so many eagles, brown pelicans, spotted owls, upland sandpipers, western pond turtles, pygmy rabbits, Oregon silverspot butterflies, et cetera—that I have to kick them out from under the bed at night. Or maybe I'd just let them stay there, where the night rustlings would sweeten my sleep.

Timing Your Visit: Bald eagles start arriving in the Klamath Basin in November, and numbers are highest in January and February. They begin leaving in March and, except for a few resident eagles, most are gone by April. The Bald Eagle Conference is always held in February.

Contact: For more information, contact Klamath Basin National Wildlife Refuges, Route 1, Box 74, Tulelake, CA 96134; (916)667-2231.

For information on the Bald Eagle Conference, contact the Oregon Department of Fish and Wildlife, 1400 Miller Island Road W., Klamath Falls, OR 97601; (503)883-5732.

Getting There: To get to the Bear Valley fly-out viewing site from Klamath Falls, drive south on Highway 97 about 14 miles to Worden. Take the first right after the grain silos, cross the railroad tracks, and take the first left onto a gravel road. Follow the road around to the right, drive about a mile, and pull over and park. The roost is straight ahead and to the right on the far timbered hill. There are houses at the end of the road; please be courteous.

To get to the Lower Klamath refuge from Klamath Falls, drive south on Highway 97 about 19 miles. Turn east into the refuge on Highway 161, which runs along the California-Oregon border. To get to refuge headquarters, located east of the refuge in California, turn south off Highway 161 onto Hill Road and go about 4 miles.

Accommodations: For information on Klamath Falls area facilities, contact the Klamath County Department of Tourism, P.O. Box 1867, Klamath Falls, OR 97601; (800)445-6728.

WHERE ELSE TO SEE WINTERING BALD EAGLES

WASHINGTON
Skagit River Bald Eagle Natural Area, northwestern Washington: Up to 300 bald eagles winter between Marblemount and Rockport along the Skagit River. Populations peak in mid-January.

To get to Skagit River Bald Eagle Natural Area from Mount Vernon, take I-5 north to Highway 20. Follow Highway 20 east to the first viewpoint about 1 mile east of Rockport. The second viewpoint is at a rest stop a little more than 1 mile farther.

For more information, contact the Nature Conservancy, 1601 Second Avenue, Suite 910, Seattle, WA 98101; (206)728-9696. For information on float trips or area facilities, contact the Marblemount Chamber of Commerce, 5879 Highway 20, Marblemount, WA 98267; (206)873-4400.

Camano Island State Park, northwestern Washington: Eagles aren't concentrated here, but they can be viewed at the park regularly during the winter.

To get to Camano Island State Park from Everett, take I-5 north to the Stanwood exit and follow Highway 532 west onto Camano Island. Take East Camano Drive and follow the signs.

For more information, contact Camano Island State Park, 2269 S. Park Road, Stanwood, WA 98292; (206)387-3031. For information on area facilities, contact the Camano Chamber of Commerce, 4008 S.W. Camano Drive, Camano Island, WA 98292; (206)387-7475.

OREGON

Twilight Eagle Sanctuary, northwestern Oregon: About forty bald eagles winter in the Twilight Creek area. A viewing platform and interpretive signs mark the site on the Columbia River.

To get to Twilight Eagle Sanctuary from Astoria, drive east on Highway 30 and exit between milepost 87 and 88. The sanctuary is located half a mile north of the highway on Burnside Road.

For more information, contact the Oregon Eagle Foundation, 5873 Estate Drive, Klamath Falls, OR 97603. For information on Astoria area facilities, contact the Astoria Chamber of Commerce, P.O. Box 176, Astoria, OR 97103; (503)325-6311.

Lewis and Clark National Wildlife Refuge, northwestern Oregon: This 15-mile-long refuge along the Columbia River is a major stopover for migrating waterfowl and the bald eagles that follow them. You really need a boat for this one.

To get to Lewis and Clark National Wildlife Refuge from Astoria, drive east on Highway 30 and watch for signs to the Brownsmead and Aldrich Point boat ramps.

For information, contact refuge headquarters, P.O. Box 566, Cathlamet, WA 98612; (206)795-3915. For Astoria area information, contact the Astoria Chamber of Commerce, P.O. Box 176, Astoria, OR 97103; (503)325-6311.

CHAPTER 19

RAM JAM

Bands of Bighorns Near Yakima, Washington

Wind stretched the big-as-a-boxcar flag in front of Perkins'
Family Restaurant so tight that there wasn't enough slack
left to flap. With luck, this same cold wind had pushed at least a
few California bighorn sheep from the high country down to
where I could see them, grazing on the steep slopes of Yakima
Canyon or eating deer chow at the Department of Wildlife's Oak
Creek sheep-feeding station.

The manager of the Oak Creek Wildlife Area—a huge expanse
of rolling range and ponderosa pine west of Yakima—said over the
phone that the winter had been so mild that sheep were keeping

to higher elevations. There were only a few around, here and there, he said. Wildlife area managers are hard to impress and sometimes forget that a few sheep will do just fine for most of us. I hung up the phone, pledged allegiance to the Ellensburg Perkins, and continued on toward Yakima Canyon.

Leaving I-90 to the rest of the world, I took exit 109, turned left at the Flying J Truck Stop, and drove straight into the cleavage of a brown-skinned Mother Earth. In its hurry, the wind didn't follow. Highway 821, the Canyon Road, snuggles beside the Yakima River for thirty-two of the most intimate miles in Washington. Once Interstate 82 was completed between Ellensburg and Yakima, travelers abandoned the old route. But driving the Canyon Road is like choosing a sit-down dinner over a Big Mac. Less convenient, but infinitely more nourishing.

Rolling along the rounded slopes of the curving canyon, moving in and out of sunlight, I watched the sparse hillside across the river for flashes of light brown: bighorn sheep—welcome familiars in Mother's private couloir. The river lay along the canyon bottom like a green satin cummerbund. Between road and riverbank, occasional stands of cottonwood trees relieved the austerity of sagebrush and dried bunchgrass.

Twenty-five million years ago this ground was flat and lush. Then cracks opened up in the earth and lava flooded the land, eventually cooling into a layer of basalt. The earth opened again many times, laying down layer after layer before it was through. This area is just part of a 200,000-square-mile lava field that spills across Washington, Oregon, and Idaho—one of the largest in the world. In some places, basalt deposits are nearly two miles thick.

Eventually, lakes, streams, and wetlands re-formed on the lava plain. Over millions of years, pressure from the earth's crust warped the basalt into hills and mountains. Land rose across the Yakima River's path, but at a slow speed that matched the river's rate of erosion. Because of this equilibrium of forces, the Yakima follows essentially the same path it always has. Sometimes on the riverbank at sunset you can hear the muttering of old voices, disguised as gurgling water and rustling leaves.

Near milepost 614, there's a little sign nailed to a tree that reads *"Bighorn pullout."* Take it as a hint.

Just south of the sign, I caught the first flash of a white rump across the river. Hidden in plain sight 200 yards away, thirty gray-brown bighorn sheep lazed and grazed on the gray-brown slope. Six rams were clustered in one group, five in another. Nineteen ewes and youngsters divided themselves into a few other bands.

A 200-pound ram got to his feet and tiptoed to a tall, bristly-looking sagebrush. He plunged his heavy, full-circle horns into the bush and scratched his head up and down. The horns of a full-grown ram can measure forty inches from skull to tip, with each one bigger around at the base than a compact disk. The full set can weigh forty pounds.

Distinct, broad bands mark sections in the horn's rippled surface. A new band, or annulus, forms each breeding season, so approximate age can be learned by counting the bands (not the ripples).

Female sheep also have horns, although theirs are much smaller and don't curl around. Rarely more than eight inches long, the ewes' horns are sickle-shaped and somewhat goatlike. The horns of a young ram and a ewe are sometimes hard to distinguish, but the male's horns are bigger at the base, more curved, and the tips are more spread out. By four years of age, a ram usually carries a three-quarter curl.

Unlike the antlers of deer and elk, which are shed and regrown annually, true horns are never dropped. The racks of old bull elk tend to grow back smaller as the animal gets older and weaker, but bighorn rams are fated to carry their bulky medallions of maleness into old age.

Another big ram joined the first, reared up on his hind legs, and fell purposefully backward onto the sagebrush. He squirmed to scratch his back. In the past, some Washington bighorns have been plagued by scabies, so I hoped this display was merely a matter of midday itch. Bighorn sheep are quite vulnerable to parasites and disease. Scabies can cause a sheep to lose its hair and subsequently die of hypothermia or some other complication.

If the sheep saw me, they gave no indication. The sentinel ewe gave no alarm; the rams were relaxed. A great blue heron flapped up from the burgundy-orange willows in the river bottom. The pleasing trilling of a meadowlark balanced the coarse *rak rak rak rak* of the magpie that was visiting a group of reclining ewes. The big black-and-white bird hopped from one unperturbed sheep to another, perching awhile on each back. Not until the brash corvid springboarded off one ewe's head was there even the slightest reaction; even then, the misused ewe merely shook her head as the—*rak rak*—magpie flew—*rak rak rak rak rak*—away.

Bighorn sheep are among the most clannish of all hoofed animals. While their group arrangements change with the season, no significant part of their lives is spent alone. Rams stick together most of the year, often in bands in which individuals are close in age. Ewes, lambs, and young rams band together, led by a matriarch who can pick the best passage over steep terrain and can find the best food, water, and shelter.

In the ram band, males are friendly until breeding season, when they get a bit testy with one another. Although rams are not as aggressively territorial with females as are bull elk, they do collect and protect harems. Mating season begins in November and lasts into December. Once the rut is over, the sheep segregate again, although several bands may share the same range. A collection of bands comprises a herd. The sheep in Yakima Canyon belong to the Umtanum herd, and the sheep near Oak Creek are part of the Clemans Mountain herd.

This was February, so the ewes nibbling grass across the way could be pregnant. Lambs are born in May or June and by winter are nearly as tall as their mothers, although they're not as heavy.

When they weren't grazing, the sheep lay chewing their cud. Cud chewing was a great evolutionary idea for animals that are the preferred quarry of meat-eating predators. For defense, the prey species must be ready to flee at the slightest hint of threat. Their metabolism can't be preoccupied with digestion when it's time to run. So, all members of the Cervidae family (deer, elk, moose, and caribou) and Bovidae family (sheep, goats, bison, and cattle) evolved as cud chewers.

A cud chewer—called a ruminant in polite circles—swallows fast when grazing and accumulates large amounts of undigested food in the first chamber of its four-part stomach. When chamber one (the rumen) is sufficiently full, the grazer retreats to a secure place to begin the next steps of digestion. The contents of the rumen are regurgitated one mouthful at a time, chewed thoroughly, and sent on to the reticulum, omasum, and abomasum. When circumstances allow, the animal chews its cud until the rumen is empty.

To balance the arguably indecorous nature of cud chewing, bighorn sheep are delicate and discriminating eaters. They consume only grasses and flowers, eschewing the woody browse of trees and shrubs that deer and elk are happy to eat.

Another car—the only one I noticed—pulled over to watch the sheep.

I would be able to tell the Oak Creek manager that I saw part of the Umtanum herd. He pitches alfalfa to hundreds of elk nearly every day in the winter, golden eagles nest across from his office, and his dog is almost smart enough to drive a stick shift. He probably wouldn't be impressed, but maybe he'd be interested.

I wound out of the canyon and onto the flat belly of the Selah Valley north of Yakima. In finding the westbound highway to Naches, I lost the river.

Bighorn sheep are native to Washington and lived in the region for an uninterrupted period from the last ice age to the early twentieth century. Rocky Mountain bighorns were native to the Selkirk and Blue mountains in the far eastern part of the state, and California bighorns lived in the Okanogan highlands and on the eastern slopes of the Cascades. The introduction of domestic livestock is thought to have been largely responsible for the disappearance of bighorns from Washington by the early 1930s.

In 1967, the Washington Department of Game (now the Department of Wildlife) released some California bighorns from a British Columbia herd onto Clemans Mountain. Subsequent releases have been made, and, although the population fluctuates, the Clemans Mountain herd now numbers about 38 animals. Washington's total bighorn population is estimated at about 750, of which 210 are the Rocky Mountain subspecies and 540 are the California subspecies. Each year the Department of Wildlife holds a drawing to determine which hunters will receive one of a small number of permits to hunt Washington's bighorns.

In normal winters, the Department of Wildlife operates a regular sheep-feeding station near Oak Creek along with its better-known elk-feeding program. But because winters have been milder than usual for several years, the need to feed bighorns has been sporadic. Nevertheless, troughs are kept full enough to keep sheep interested.

Positioned behind a tall wire fence and tucked into the base of Clemans Mountain, the sheep-feeding station is an open corral with a few troughs in it. No sheep were in the corral when I got there, but a scan of the hillside showed a ram band and one loose ewe picking their way single file down the slope.

The cloven hooves of wild sheep are like rubbery pads. Dew claws in back serve as brakes. A 200-pound ram with 40-pound horns can negotiate any surface that can offer two-inch footholds five or six feet apart going up, and not more than twenty feet apart going down. Sheep are "bounders" as opposed to mountain goats, which are climbers.

Many other clear distinctions exist between bighorn sheep and mountain goats. Mountain goats have straight, pointed black horns, black hooves, shaggy white coats, and natty goatees. Unlike bighorns, which can be found in the desert, mountain goats rarely stray outside the alpine environment.

The rams and ewe paused outside the corral for a minute before they walked in. As long as you are quiet and move slowly, the sheep will tolerate your presence at the fence. They ate daintily, lips rustling through the pellets in the long wooden troughs.

Considering how social they are, bighorn sheep are uncommonly quiet. When the elk are being fed over at Oak Creek, the yard is full of mews, snorts, grunts, and whistles. The sheep were silent.

I wondered what the ewe was doing there. The breeding season was long over, but one of the rams seemed to be squiring her around anyway. I suppose some males know no season.

With their heavy horns, elegant Roman noses, and dispassionate poise, bighorn sheep have the air of mythological creatures. The impression is furthered by the fact that it's hard to look them in the eye. Bighorns have huge, black, rectangular pupils that are set in their yellow eyes like gun ports, leaving you feeling as though they're looking through you, not at you.

After a while the sheep wandered out of the corral and began to graze their way up the hill.

Craaack!

While most of the band had gone on, two rams held back to relieve a minor rush of testosterone. They squared off about twenty-five feet from each other, reared up on their hind legs, paused a second or two, and then leaned full speed into the charge—running on their hind legs before the final lunge.

Craaack!

The rams staggered back a few steps. If this were a cartoon, planets, stars, and tweetie birds would be circling their heads, and their eyes would be little Xs. After a pause to regain their senses, they reared again.

Craaack!

The sound of the twenty-mile-per-hour head-on can be heard for two miles—the origin of the word *ramming* revealed at last.

Today's bout was low key. If this had been the breeding season, there would have been pawing, snorting, groaning, and glaring, plus maybe some bleeding and broken horn tips. Several Clemans Mountain rams carried wide scars like bandoliers across their shoulders and chests. Breeding season battles may be as short as a few minutes or as long as two to three hours. But even though the fighting is for real, rams seem to retain some sense of fraternity, especially with males of their own band. Sideline rams watch the match and have been known to trade off with the principal participants. Sometimes, when the battle is over, combatants walk away together. Maybe it's because they're so dizzy they can't remember what the problem was, or who was fighting with whom.

After three rounds, the two rams lost interest and turned up the hill after the others.

I headed for home too, back through the Yakima Canyon, where evening was turning the landscape into layered silhouettes. All too soon, I emerged from the canyon's curvy cleavage and accelerated into the westbound traffic of I-90. The straight interstate was dull after being rocked by the loose meander of road-along-river and entranced by the transcendental spiral of ram horns. Images of those heavy, helixed horns stayed with me all the way back to sheepless Puget Sound.

I think Mother must have designated bighorns as the standard-bearers for her most essential pattern. They're not sheep—they're walking whirlpools.

Timing Your Visit: Snow and cold weather are the keys, but generally, January, February, and March are good months to see sheep in Yakima Canyon and at Oak Creek.

Contact: For more information on bighorn sheep in the Oak Creek Wildlife Area, contact the Washington Department of Wildlife, 2802 Fruitvale Boulevard, Yakima, WA 98902-1190; (509)575-2740.

Getting There: To get to Canyon Road (Highway 821) from Ellensburg, take I-90 east a few miles to exit 109 and follow signs. From Yakima, take exit 26 off I-82 and follow signs.

To get to the Oak Creek sheep-feeding station from Yakima, take Highway 12 west through Naches. About 4 miles past Naches, just this side of the Highway 410 junction, turn right onto the old Naches Highway. The corral and gravel parking area are close by on the left. (*Note:* Highway 410 is closed at Chinook Pass in the winter.)

Accommodations: For information on area facilities, contact the South Central Washington Tourism Council, P.O. Box 1490, Yakima, WA 98907; (509)248-2021.

WHERE ELSE TO SEE BIGHORN SHEEP

WASHINGTON
Sullivan Lake, northeastern Washington: Sheep are generally at the Sullivan Lake sheep-feeding station from December until late February. Visitors must walk uphill a quarter-mile from the parking area, or farther if the road to the parking area isn't plowed.

To get to the Sullivan Lake sheep-feeding area from Spokane, take Highway 2, then Highway 211, and then Highway 20 north to Tiger. A few miles farther up the road, just south of Ione, head east over the Pend Oreille River and continue on Sullivan Lake Road about 8 miles. Turn east on the Noisy Creek campground road and park near the closed gate.

For more information on the Sullivan Lake sheep-feeding program, contact the Department of Wildlife, N. 8702 Division Street, Spokane, WA 99218; (509)456-4082. For information on area facilities, contact the Ione Chamber of Commerce, P.O. Box 518, Ione, WA 99139; (509)442-3737.

Sinlahekin Wildlife Area, north-central Washington: Sinlahekin received the state's first bighorn reintroductions in 1957, and the herd has done well; there is no feeding station here. Before you go, call for road conditions; access can be difficult in this remote area.

To get to Sinlahekin Wildlife Area from Omak, take Highway 97/20 north. A little more than 5 miles north of Riverside, turn west onto Pine Creek Road. Pine Creek Road turns into Fish Lake Road, which turns into Sinlahekin Road. The wildlife area is a few miles north of Fish Lake on the east side of the road. Use an Okanogan Forest Service map to find your way.

For more information on Sinlahekin Wildlife Area, contact the Department of Wildlife, P.O. Box 850, Ephrata, WA 98823; (509)754-4624. For maps, contact the Okanogan National Forest, P.O. Box 950, Okanogan, WA 98840; (509)422-2704. For information on area facilities, contact the Omak Chamber of Commerce, P.O. Box 2087, Omak, WA 98841; (509)826-1880.

OREGON

Wenaha Wildlife Area, northeastern Oregon: Bighorn sheep winter in this wildlife area situated along the Grande Ronde and Wenaha rivers. Call ahead for road conditions and viewing advice.

To get to Wenaha Wildlife Area from Enterprise, take Highway 3 north. In about 35 miles, turn west toward Flora and follow the steep gravel road 14 miles to wildlife area headquarters in Troy. Logging trucks can make the route dangerous in winter; so, for a safer route, continue on Highway 3 into Washington (where Highway 3 turns into Highway 129) and, just after crossing the Grande Ronde River, turn left onto Grande Ronde Road back down to Troy.

For more information on Wenaha Wildlife Area, contact the Oregon Department of Fish and Wildlife, Route 2, Box 2283, La Grande, OR 97850; (503)963-2138. For information on area facilities, contact the Wallowa County Chamber of Commerce, P.O. Box 427, Enterprise, OR 97828; (503)426-4622.

Hart Mountain National Antelope Refuge, southeastern Oregon:
Poker Jim Ridge is a good place to look for bighorn sheep in this
remote area. Call ahead for road conditions and viewing advice.

To get to Hart Mountain Antelope Refuge from Bend, go
south on Highway 97 and turn southeast onto Highway 31 just
south of LaPine. Take Highway 31 to just north of Lakeview and
turn east onto Highway 140. At Adel, drive northeast to Plush.
Refuge headquarters is another 25 miles to the northeast.

For more information on Hart Mountain, contact refuge
headquarters, P.O. Box 111, Lakeview, OR 97630; (503)947-
3315. For information on area facilities, contact Lake County
Chamber of Commerce, Courthouse, Lakeview, OR 97630-1577;
(503)947-6040.

CHAPTER 20

GRAY DAYS

Whale Watch Week on the Central Oregon Coast,
Oregon

Putu, Siku, and Kanik ("Ice Hole," "Ice," and "Snowflake") were paying for a serious error in judgment. It was late October of 1988 and the three gray whales should have been on their way to Baja for the winter. Instead, the tardy migrants were trapped by the closing polar ice pack near Point Barrow, Alaska. As the world looked on, a million dollars' worth of helicopters and heavy equipment was put to the task of carving an escape route through the ice to free the struggling whales.

The event exposed just how completely whales can pick the

lock of a human heart. They are like dreams that we can see, smell, and hear—real, yet mysterious, and tantalizingly beyond our reach.

While we know relatively little about the intimacies of a gray whale's life, we do know that the whales migrate along the Washington and Oregon coasts between November and February every year without fail. Also every year without fail, Oregon holds Whale Watch Week to celebrate the whales as they travel by on their way from feeding grounds in the Bering and Chukchi seas off Alaska to breeding and calving grounds off Baja, Mexico. Always held the week between Christmas and New Year's, Whale Watch Week is timed to coincide with the peak of the southward migration, when up to thirty whales an hour may be seen passing Pacific Coast headlands. It's the ultimate New Year's parade. As part of the holiday ritual, I make a resolution for every whale I see going by. If they can swim from Alaska to Baja and back in one year, I can read more books, be more loving, and cut back on fat, sugar, and salt.

Blue-and-white "Whale Watching Spoken Here" signs draw visitors to more than thirty volunteer-staffed viewpoints all along the Oregon coast. Calm, overcast mornings are the best time to look for whales. Whitecaps often blow up later in the day, making it hard to spot a spout, and glaring sun can obscure vision. Fort Stevens near Astoria, Cape Foulweather near Newport, and Cape Perpetua near Florence are three of the more accessible viewing sites. Newport's Mark O. Hatfield Marine Science Center, which coordinates Whale Watch Week, can provide a list of designated viewpoints and offers daily films, talks, and gray whale show-and-tell.

If you crave more than a cliffside seat, as little as eight dollars buys a chance to slip out to sea and cruise with the whales for an hour or so. More money buys more time. Throughout the winter gray migration, which begins slowly in late November and is basically over by early February, tour operators in several coastal towns offer a variety of charter opportunities.

At Depoe Bay, whale-watching boats leave the self-proclaimed smallest harbor in the world through a snaking, 100-yard-long cleft in the rocks. Passage through the heaving, kelp-lined channel is just a warm-up for the rocking ride over the bar. (A "bar" is the naturally formed underwater sandbar found at the mouths of many harbors and rivers. The water over it is shallower, and so is especially rough. Among fishermen, "crossing the bar" is a euphemism for dying—except in Ketchikan, Alaska, where "crossing the bar" means punching the bartender.)

On one particular day of Whale Watch Week, I set out through the channel with nine other souls in search of a waking dream: to see, hear, smell, and simply be in the same acre of ocean with a forty-five-foot gray whale. In town, clouds were heavy, but the fifty-degree air felt balmy for the second day after Christmas. Out on the water, however, the wind picked up and the temperature dropped.

Steering the fifty-foot *Kingfisher* from its open-air flying bridge, smiling and looking soul-satisfied with his place in the world, Captain Dan "Boonskee" Zimmerman gave us a little background over the loudspeaker. Gray whales complete the longest migration of any mammal, nearly 10,000 miles round trip. Grays, he said encouragingly, are the most frequently seen whale off the West Coast.

A young deckhand craned his neck scanning the horizon for a "blow," the telltale spout of vapor exhaled by a surfacing whale. Seven hopeful whale watchers clung to the tall bow rail, listening to the skipper and bending their knees as the boat rolled with the swells. Two, more nonchalant, passengers drank steamy, sloshing coffee in the cabin. A tall, green-faced boy was already tucked up on a bench by the galley table, no doubt praying for the tossing boat to turn around.

Boonskee continued.

The trip from the Bering Sea to Baja takes about three months, and pregnant females are first to leave in the fall (making it a good bet that Putu, Siku, and Kanik weren't expecting). The cows travel singly, in pairs, or in trios, and have the fastest travel time. Adult males and nonpregnant females leave next, traveling in groups of up to twelve. Immature animals generally bring up the rear. Besides having a reputation for poky behavior, subadult whales are also known to digress occasionally from the straight-ahead migration route to explore such roadside attractions as the inside waters of Puget Sound in Washington, and the islands off southern California.

Gray whales generally stay within one-half to two miles of shore. At one time, this near-shore migration and the whales' habit of collecting in a few select lagoons in Baja made them easy prey for whalers. In the mid-1800s, whaling captain Charles Scammon diligently described the species even as he decimated them on their breeding grounds. These days, however, the grays are in more sympathetic company.

"Thar she blows!" yelled the deckhand, slapping off and on a red baseball cap. He showed no signs of embarrassment at the shouted cliché.

On whale-watching boats, the first sighting of a whale is like an orchestra conductor's tap of the baton. Before a sighting, there's a lot of every-which-way conversation and laughter, like instruments tuning up. But as soon as someone points, attention immediately becomes focused.

"I see it!" (Tap, tap, tap.)

"Where?" (The word draws out like a bow over violin strings.)

"There! There! Over There!" (The brass comes in.)

"I still don't see it." (Piccolos.)

"There! There!" (Reaching toward crescendo—)

"Oh! Oh! Yes! Yes!" (Triumphant finale, Symphony in See.)

Captain Boonskee turned the *Kingfisher* in the direction of the blow.

Being able to spot spouts is crucial to successful whale watching, whether you're standing on a bluff or on a boat. First, scan the ocean's surface without binoculars. Look below the horizon for twelve- to fifteen-foot plumes of vapor that look something like the smoke from a cannon. Once you've spotted a blow, use the binoculars to focus in.

Astute observers have noticed that gray whales blow three to five times in a row, about thirty to fifty seconds apart, before they "sound," or dive deeply. If a whale raises its tail flukes straight up before it dives, that's a good clue it's sounding. In deep dives, whales may stay underwater for up to ten minutes. Gray whales don't dive as deeply as other whales, but they do make long dives of up to several minutes during migration. *The Oceanic Society Field Guide to the Gray Whale* explains that, as a rule of thumb, you can expect a gray to blow once for each minute it has spent in a dive. Whalers called this "having his spoutings out." The

Oceanic Society guide suggests using a second hand or stop-watch to time the blows in order to predict when the whale will surface next.

If you can, get downwind of the spouts; if you dare, that is. Whale breath has been described as smelling like a mix of bad fish and sump oil. An entry in an old whaling text declares the breath of a whale to be "so insupportably smelly that it brings on disorders of the brain." It could be true. My old dog, Cisco, who used to troll for salmon with me in Southeast Alaska, would go berserk whenever she smelled whales. She jumped overboard twice in whale-breath frenzies. Lucky for her the whales were of the baleen variety.

The order Cetacea is divided into toothed whales and baleen whales. Toothed whales, which include orcas (killer whales), sperm whales, dolphins, and porpoises, are the larger group by far. Orcas are known to sometimes eat not only fish but marine mammals, including seals and baby gray whales. One recent report had them attacking a swimming moose. I don't know if they eat dogs.

Baleen whales, including grays, bowheads, and humpbacks, feed mostly on tiny shrimplike organisms called amphipods and other small crustaceans known collectively as krill. Most of what are referred to as the great whales—cetaceans over twenty-five feet—are baleen whales. This translates poetically into the fact that the planet's largest animals eat some of the planet's smallest.

The baleen whale has from 200 to 400 long, narrow strips, or "plates," of baleen growing from its upper gumline. Each one measures several inches across at the top and tapers down to a point. These plates, which can be from less than a foot to nearly fourteen feet long, hang down like partially drawn vertical blinds. One edge of the strip is frayed along its whole length in order to snare the krill. When a baleen whale feeds, it takes in large volumes of water and then uses its Volkswagen-size tongue to push the water out through the screen, leaving just krill and sometimes small fish trapped inside its mouth.

baleen

Baleen is made of keratin—the same strong, pliable, durable substance that forms hair, hooves, horns, and fingernails. Before the advent of petroleum products, baleen was used in essentially the same way plastic is used today. Called "whalebone," baleen was once used for corset frames, collar stays, umbrella ribs, and buggy whips. Native peoples of the Arctic use baleen to weave baskets.

The baleen of gray whales is particularly strong because grays dredge their food from the sea floor instead of screening it out of the water column. Grays (probably young ones) sometimes wander into northern Puget Sound to feed in Saratoga Passage and Port Susan. When whales are in the area, low tide exposes a profusion of six-inch-deep, ten-foot-wide pits created by the whales' feeding activities. Sand piles alongside the depressions are the whale's tailings. These feeding youngsters are the exception; most whales don't eat during the southward migration, although they are often seen snacking on the return trip north.

"Most grays don't eat once they leave the Arctic," explained Captain Boonskee. "They head south with a foot-thick layer of blubber and may not eat again until they head back north six months later. A whale may lose one-third of its body weight during that time."

We were approaching the spouting whale, and Captain Boonskee followed proper whale-watching etiquette by slowing the boat while still a respectful distance off. He kept the gray to our right and paralleled its course at a fraction of a knot slower so as not to disturb it or cause it to change direction.

PUUSSSHHHHhhhhhhhh. During the two long seconds it took for the whale to clear its substantial lungs, the top of its head was clearly visible. A deep, breathing-in sound followed, drawing an aural picture of the air-breathing giant just below the surface. Excited whale watchers crowded the starboard rail, imaginations drawn into the sea as the boat jogged south with the cruising whale.

The gray scooped more shallow dives, breathing out and in, exposing a length that nearly matched the fifty-foot boat. Encrustations of barnacles and huge splotches of light scar tissue mottled its dark skin like storm clouds shattered against an overcast sky. We watched as the "knuckles" on its dorsal ridge rolled forward into the sea a good second or two ahead of its twelve-foot tail flukes.

With each scoop, the gray left its "footprint," a glassy swirl on the water's surface. Couples drew closer and children worked their way under parents' arms. Everyone was smiling, except the boy below, who probably hated whales by this time and never wanted to see one as long as he lived.

While we shivered and bobbed on the wooden boat, praising our time-release motion-sickness skin patches and acupressure bracelets, and sharing capsules of ginger and other seasickness home remedies, the whale was totally at home in the cold, broad ocean. It wasn't always so.

Whales were once land animals. Fossil evidence as well as bio-chemical and genetic studies support the idea that cetaceans evolved from hoofed mammals. It's interesting to think that, while all life came from the sea, at some point certain life forms decided they'd had enough and went back. Front limbs adapted into flippers, nostrils migrated to the top of the head, and external ears disappeared. And once free of gravity's restraint, whales picked up on their option to grow larger and larger. Whale skeletons on display at the Hatfield Marine Science Center show vestigial hind limbs and ball-and-socket shoulder joints.

All that evolution was nearly for naught. Right whales (so named because they were the "right" whale to kill), bowheads, humpbacks, sperm whales, grays, and others were nearly wiped out by whalers in the late nineteenth and early twentieth centuries. Human beings have hunted whales from the earliest of times, but modern whaling, considered to have begun in 1864 with advances in technology, nearly closed the book. For decades, tens of thousands of whales were caught and processed annually by oceangoing factory ships and efficient shore stations.

Some protection was attempted as early as the 1930s, and whaling has been heavily regulated and whales further protected since at least the 1960s. Under the security of international protection, the gray whale has made a remarkable comeback. The current estimate of 21,000 individuals is thought to exceed pre-exploitation levels. Another factor working in their favor is the fact that regular migration habits in a narrow range make it relatively easy for the whales to find reproductive partners. Male and female baleen whales don't form long-term bonds; after mating, the two have no more to do with each other. Mothers and calves comprise the basic social unit. (Toothed whales are more gregarious and form long-lasting extended family groups.)

Our hour was up, and Captain Boonskee turned the *Kingfisher* east, leaving the gray to go on alone. Nine souls—cold and thrilled, noses dripping with sea spray—gathered on the back deck. Several spoke of plans to go out again the next day. They were determined to see a whale breach—leap way out of the water and splash back down on its back or side. We had heard that, the day before, passengers on another boat had watched one whale fling itself mightily out of the water five times in a row.

Cisco and I used to see whales breach while we were fishing. The awesome sight left us grasping for ways to express our own exuberance. Cisco would run scrambling laps around our thirty-six-foot boat, and I would climb onto the top of the wheelhouse and hoot for more, knees shaking. Our partner Tim would dash for the camera.

I hoped these elated whale watchers really would go back out—and would keep going out until they were witness to the Symphony in See, Major.

Timing Your Visit: Southbound migrating gray whales begin to appear off the Washington and Oregon coasts in late November. Numbers peak around the last week of December. Whales return north in late March in a less concentrated procession.

Contact: For more information on Whale Watch Week or whales in the Northwest, contact the Oregon State University Mark O. Hatfield Marine Science Center, 2030 S. Marine Science Drive, Newport, OR 97365; (503)867-0100.

Getting There: To get to the Mark O. Hatfield Marine Science Center, which is on the southern outskirts of Newport, take the Marine Science Center exit off Highway 101 just south of the Yaquina Bay Bridge.

To get to Depoe Bay from Newport, take Highway 101 north about 14 miles to Depoe Bay.

Accommodations and Charters: For information on area facilities and charters, contact the Depoe Bay Chamber of Commerce, P.O. Box 21, Depoe Bay, OR 97341; (503)765-2889. Or contact the Greater Newport Chamber of Commerce, 555 S.W. Coast

Highway, Newport, OR 97365; (800)262-7844.

WHERE ELSE TO SEE GRAY WHALES

WASHINGTON

Cape Alava, Olympic Peninsula, Washington: A well-traveled foot trail not quite four miles long leads from the road to this excellent viewpoint on the outer coast of Washington. Walk in only.

To get to Cape Alava from Port Angeles, take Highway 112 west to the Ozette turnoff about 2 miles past Sekiu.

For more information on Cape Alava, contact Olympic National Park, 600 E. Park Avenue, Port Angeles, WA 98362; (206)452-4501. For information on area facilities, contact the Peninsula Tourism Council, 120 Washington, Suite 101-A, Bremerton, WA 98310; (800)433-7828, ext. 30.

Westport Viewing Tower, southwestern Washington: If beach hikes and boat rides aren't for you, drive right up to Westport's 50-foot viewing tower. Afterward, visit the whale exhibit.

To get to Westport from Aberdeen, dogleg south on Highway 101 for about a mile, and then follow Highway 105 west.

For more information on the viewing tower and on area facilities, contact the Westport/Grayland Chamber of Commerce, P.O. Box 306, Westport, WA 98595; (800)345-6223.

OREGON

Cape Lookout State Park, northern coast, Oregon: The 5-mile hike to the cape lookout is well worth the trouble. Besides whales, peregrine falcons are also sometimes seen in the area.

To get to Cape Lookout from Tillamook, take the Netarts Highway west and south about 7 miles to Whiskey Creek Road. Turn south; Whiskey Creek Road turns into Cape Lookout Road. Follow signs to the parking area and trailhead.

For more information on the park, contact Cape Lookout State Park, 13000 Whiskey Creek Road W., Tillamook, OR 97141; (503)842-4981. For information on area facilities, contact the Tillamook Chamber of Commerce, 3705 Highway 101 N., Tillamook, OR 97141; (503)842-7525.

Cape Sebastian State Park, southern coast, Oregon: Cape Sebastian's 700-foot-high headland offers an excellent vantage point for whale watching. A steep trail leads down to the beach for further exploration.

To get to Cape Sebastian from Eugene, take Highway 126 west to U.S. Highway 101 and turn south. Cape Sebastian is about 85 miles south of Coos Bay.

For more information on the park, contact Oregon State Parks, 1155 S. 5th Street, Coos Bay, OR 97420; (503)269-9410. For information on area facilities, contact the Brookings–Harbor Chamber of Commerce, P.O. Box 940, Brookings, OR 97415; (503)469-3181.

ACKNOWLEDGMENTS

Going Wild is natural history without the museum—biology with its feet up on the desk. It's hard to draw a clean academic line between humans and animals when we share so many of the same basic needs and drives; so I don't. Both humans and animals need air, water, food, space, and a safe place to rest, court, and raise young. I believe we have more in common with animals than not, especially if you look at the big picture.

As this isn't the traditional perspective taken by biological science, I doubly appreciate the comments, corrections, and clarifications offered by the wildlife experts who reviewed this manuscript. They were tolerant of my nonscientific tangents and generous in their willingness to help me get the details of natural history correct. If inaccuracies persist, they are my responsibility.

For their time and effort, I thank Louise Accurso, Deanne Converse, David Denning, Laurel Devaney, Judy Friesem, Ron Friesz, John Garrett, Don Giles, E. Ron Harding, Steve Haydock, Bill Hesselbart, Gary Ivey, Kelly McAlister, John McGowan, Dave Menke, Bruce Moorhead, Woody Myers, Robin Norris, Robert Michael Pyle, Susan Riemer, Jim Runkles, Mike Smith, and David Weiss.

In addition, I appreciate the cheerful assistance offered by many unnamed rangers, biologists, office staffers, and others who answered questions, sent information, and volunteered suggestions based on their own experiences. When there was no one to ask, I went to the library, which is full of excellent resources on Northwest plants and animals. A few of my favorite reference works are listed in the back of this book; also included in that list are other sources cited in the text.

It was a privilege and pleasure to work with editors Ellen Wheat and Linda Gunnarson. They let me be me, only better. Sincere thanks also goes to the rest of the Alaska Northwest Books staff, who knew what to do and did it. I'm obliged to Gretchen Daiber—without her illustrations, *Going Wild* would be like a house with no windows. And thanks to Pat, for his understanding and support.

RELATED READING

Bellrose, Frank C. *Ducks, Geese and Swans of North America,* 3d Ed. Harrisburg, Penn.: Stackpole Books, 1980.

Bennett, Ben. *The Oceanic Society Field Guide to the Gray Whale.* Seattle: Sasquatch Books, 1989.

Benyus, Janine M. *The Field Guide to Wildlife Habitats of the Western United States.* New York: Simon & Schuster, 1989.

Clark, Ella E. *Indian Legends of the Pacific Northwest.* Berkeley: University of California Press, 1953.

Erdoes, Richard, and Alfonso Ortiz, eds. *American Indian Myths and Legends.* New York: Random House, 1984.

Goodnight, Julie, and Sara Vickerman. *Oregon Wildlife Viewing Guide.* Portland, Ore.: Defenders of Wildlife, 1988.

Ingles, Lloyd G. *Mammals of the Pacific States.* Stanford, Calif.: Stanford University Press, 1965.

Kozloff, Eugene N. *Seashore Life of the Northern Pacific Coast.* Seattle: University of Washington Press, 1983.

Kruckeberg, Arthur. *The Natural History of Puget Sound Country.* Seattle: University of Washington Press, 1991.

La Tourrette, Joe. *Washington Wildlife Viewing Guide.* Helena, Mont.: Falcon Press, 1992.

Littlefield, Carroll D. *Birds of Malheur National Wildlife Refuge.* Corvallis: Oregon State University Press, 1990.

Mathews, Daniel. *Cascade–Olympic Natural History.* Portland, Ore.: Raven Editions, 1988.

Nussbaum, Ronald A., Edmund D. Brodie, Jr., and Robert M. Storm. *Amphibians and Reptiles of the Pacific Northwest.* Moscow: University of Idaho Press, 1983.

Oregon/Washington Watchable Wildlife. Portland, Ore.: Bureau of Land Management, 1991.

Pyle, Robert Michael. *Handbook for Butterfly Watchers.* Boston: Houghton Mifflin, 1992.

Tuttle, Merlin D. *America's Neighborhood Bats.* Austin: University of Texas Press, 1988.

INDEX